Caucasian Shepherd

Caucasian Ovcha

What you must know before you buy a Caucasian Shepherd Dog / Caucasian Ovcharka as a Pet.

by

Clifford Worthington

Published by: IMB Publishing

Table of Contents

Table of Contents 3

Chapter 1. Dogs as Pets 7

Chapter 2. Introducing the Caucasian Shepherd 10

1. Useful Facts about the Caucasian Shepherd Dog...................... 11

2. History of the Breed 13

3. Description of dogs with different origins 15

4. Appearance of Caucasian Shepherd Dogs................................. 16
    a.   Features 16
    b.   Colors... 16
    c.   Height and Weight... 17
    d.   Life Expectancy 17

Chapter 3. Buying a Caucasian Shepherd Dog 18

1. Asking for Papers 18

2. Know the Basics 20
    a. Personality and temperament of the Caucasian Shepherd............... 20
    b. Age 20
    c. Gender 21
    d. Number 21

3. How to Ensure You Are Buying a Healthy One? 21
    a. Shot Records and Vaccinations 22
    b. Dew Claws 22

4. Questions to ask the breeder 23

5. Where to Buy and For How Much? 25
    a. How do you know which breeder is good? 25
    b. Where to buy the dog in the US?.. 26

Table of Contents

c. How much do they cost in US?.. 28

d. Where to buy the dog in the UK?... 28

e. How much do they cost in UK? 29

6. Registry of a CS... 29

7. Educate Yourself... 29

Chapter 4. What to Expect Post Purchase **31**

1. The Adjustment Stage.. 31

2. Compatibility with co-inhabitants :.. 32

3. Lifespan and Size.. 33

4. How to Bond with Your Caucasian Shepherd 33

5. Pros and Cons of Owning a Caucasian Shepherd 34

Chapter 5. How To Take Care of A Caucasian Shepherd **36**

1. Grooming 36

   a. Coat 36

   b. Proper way of Brushing 37

   c. Dew Claws 38

   d. Nail Trimming: 39

   e. Ear Care: 40

   f. Bathing: 40

2. Tail Docking... 41

3. Worming 41

4. Feeding... 44

   a. Types of Diets for Dogs.. 44

   b. The Caucasian Shepherd's Diet 45

   c. What to Feed At 3 months: 46

   d. Feeding an adult dog:... 48

   e. Gravity Fed Feeders.. 48

   f. Pro Plan 48

   g. Foods to Avoid 49

Table of Contents

h. Dog Treats 50

5. Accommodation 51

6. Setting the Rules 53

7. Transporting 54

8. Possible Illnesses and Plan of Action 55

9. Training 55
   a. Phases of Dog Training 57
   b. Teaching tricks to your dog 58
   c. How Teaching Tricks to Your Dog Will Help You 68
   d. Points to Be Wary Of 69
   e. How to make your dog listen to you? 70

10. Breeding 71

11. Walking 73

12. Socializing 73

13. Poison Control 77
   a. Inside Plants 78
   b. Outside Plants: 78
   c. Human Foods: 79
   d. Miscellaneous 80
   e. Hazards for Dogs during the Holidays 81
   f. Signs of toxicity 81
   g. What to do in case of suspected dog poisoning? 82
   f. Poison-protection: Pet-proofing your Home 82

14. Spaying and Neutering 83
   a. When to get it done? 83
   b. Why do it? 83
   c. What are the behavioral and health benefits related to these procedures? 84
   d. But it costs too much! 84
   e. Not even one litter for my purebred? 84
   f. If I find them a home, then its okay, right? 85

Table of Contents

g. So my female dog cannot even have one litter? 85

h. Does neutering change the personality of the pet? 85

Chapter 6. Annual Cost of Keeping a Caucasian Shepherd **86**

Chapter 7. Some General How-Tos **88**

1. Potty-Train Your Dog *88*

a. Things to know before potty training 88

b. Potty Training a Puppy 90

c. Potty Training an Adult Caucasian Mountain Dog 90

2. Take Care of Pregnant Female Dogs *90*

a. What to Feed your Pregnant Dog? 92

b. Whelping 92

3. Take Care of Newborn Puppies *97*

4. Take Care of an Aging Dog *110*

5. Prevent Them from Escaping *112*

6. What to do when the dog attacks someone? *114*

Territorial Aggression: 114

Predatory Aggression: 115

What to do when your dog does bite? 115

Some Useful Websites **117**

Useful Checklists **119**

Conclusion **121**

Chapter 1. Dogs as Pets

It is no news that dogs make excellent pets. They are loyal, intelligent, affectionate, and even gifted in a lot of ways. A lot of people have benefitted from keeping dogs as pets in a myriad of ways. Some say they provide excellent company, while others claim that they portray a sense of unconditional love and acceptance for their owners, the sort that cannot even be expected from a fellow human. The more conventional, if you may, approach is to keep them to guard your property like your home or farm, while some epileptic patients keep them to be alerted of an eminent attack. Such dogs are called seizure alert dogs or seizure response dogs.

Dogs may help their owners stay healthy in many other ways. Being with a dog helps shed stress and strains from everyday life because the love and comfort you get from a faithful companion is sometimes all you need after a long and demanding day. Dog owners are also said to have stronger immune systems and can therefore keep illnesses away. Dogs also help keep the owner's blood pressure low simply by being petted and also help you recover faster from a personal trauma.

It is also believed that people who own dogs have a faster rate of recovery from illnesses and have a higher chance of surviving a heart attack. If you have children, then keeping a dog is great because they help build self esteem in children; instill a love for animals and a sense of responsibility by taking care of another living being and also provide them the companionship which is unparalleled via other animals.

This book is about the Caucasian Shepherd – a ferocious but loyal guard dog. You may have seen it many times, and it may seem like a cuddly thing. But in reality, it is an aggressive one, and this book attempts to show people how to actually care for it. But first, we will give a brief introduction about what the general needs of having a dog as a pet are, and that should determine the kind you should get. Caucasian Shepherds are a tough breed to pet and they will have their own set of requirements that you will read about in the later part of the book.

The Needs of a Pet

This is an important factor that should determine your choice when purchasing a dog. We take the utmost care of our vehicles, which makes caring for our pets even more important since they are living creatures like us. So what are the major needs of a dog?

Grooming

Some dogs shed naturally and as such they don't need grooming. Of course, you need to bathe them regularly, but the hassle of having their hair cut is removed. But in the case of a dog breed like the Poodle, grooming is an important component of the whole pet ownership experience.

For the most part, dog owners go to specialists for having their dogs groomed. This is an additional expense, and will continue for as long as you own your pet. Keep this factor in mind.

Consider your Housing Capacity

You may want a dog that your kids can play with, and it is fun playing Frisbee with a pet. The only issue is that you need a large space to do so. You should either have a garden of your own, or you should have a park near your residence. If that is not the case, then you should consider going for something like a Labrador or a Caucasian Shepherd.

Go with a smaller breed if you live in an apartment building. There are many people who own breeds like the pit bull, but they have no space to keep them in their apartments.

In these situations, the pets are either locked away in a small space with minimal movement, or the owner has to rent or purchase another place just to accommodate the dogs. Do not make this mistake.

Healthcare

This cannot be stressed enough. Diseases are not rare among animals, especially dogs. It is not just important to buy a healthy breed, but you also need to know when to take the pet for vaccination. Once again, the money factor comes into play here as animal medication and veterinary services are not cheap.

Food/Monetary aspects

Obviously, your dog will require food and water. However, the type of breed you choose does influence how much food you need to buy. Larger dogs will naturally eat more food, so you have to make sure whether you can handle this or not. Even with a smaller breed, you need to spend at least thirty-five dollars (twenty pounds) on food, but this can last over several months. One thing related to food is the defecation process. In simple terms, the more they eat, the more they poop. So even if you can afford to purchase and feed a large dog, be prepared to do a lot of cleaning! Make sure you have money to feed your dog

Chapter 2. Introducing the Caucasian Shepherd

What one firstly needs to know is that the Caucasian Shepherd **is not an ideal family pet!** The main reason for me writing this book is because my neighbor's Caucasian Shepherd attacked one of their friends, visiting their house and the friend was very badly injured. It *could* well be that your Caucasian Shepherd is a loving dog but that's also what my neighbor thought until their dog attacked their friend.

WORD OF WARNING: NEVER LEAVE A CAUSIAN SHEPHERSD ALONE WITH A CHILD. You should never leave a child on it's own with ANY dog anyway.

It is mostly used for guarding purposes, for large commercial estates, the Military and prison. The application of this dog can be ascribed to its strong willed, ferocious and fearless nature. It is also very loyal and will protect anything and anyone it considers his family, including other dogs, children and even cats. But know that it **will attack everyone else**. This may include friends of your children and any guests who may visit you.

Also, this dog is **not for anyone who is planning to get a dog for the very first time**. This is for those experienced dog lovers who have the time, passion and expertise to tame, train and socialize this aggressive breed.

This dog *might* not be your delightful playmate. Your dog *might* not like tricks and play fetch with you. The Caucasian Shepherd will be happy if and when he can do the job he is born and trained to do, i.e. to guard and protect.

If you have cared well for this dog, had it well socialized, put in a lot of patience and attention in his training, then you can expect him to be highly loyal and devoted, giving you a complete peace of mind. But you need to ensure that this one is a working breed and needs to have a guarding job to keep him busy. They are now increasingly being owned by people to guard their property and to deter inmates in prison.

1. Useful Facts about the Caucasian Shepherd Dog

There are some useful facts about the Caucasian Shepherd Dog that might prove to be helpful should you choose to own one. There might also be myth busters of sorts, since there is a lot of controversy surrounding this one particular breed.

1- The Caucasian Shepherd is **not inherently dangerous**. It has been used to guard flocks of animals for hundreds of years, and because of its build and strength, it can bring down bears and wolves if necessary. But they would never attack the animal it is supposed to be protecting. This applies not only to animals, but also to the family that owns it, and has trained it to protect.

2- The Caucasian Shepherd is not **a typical family pet**. It can live in a human family, but it will not act as a play mate or a cuddly pet. It can be seen chasing children around because it has an inherent herding instinct, and only tries to keep them in the flock. It does not in any way mean that it will attack children of the family. **Any strangers will be attacked**. The herding instinct and assault on strangers sometimes leads to startling the smaller children, which eventually surprises the dog and makes it aggressive.

11

Therefore, **families with small children are not recommended to pet this dog.**

3- You can totally **get this dog** if you are **not a first time dog owner**. You need to keep the alpha role with yourself and have a lot of experience in taming dogs. A strong physique will also help handle this big dog. You will also need to get this dog to exercise pretty often, so only own one if you are willing and able to commit so much time to it.

4- The **Caucasian Shepherd makes a great protector**. It has protective instincts so it will not need any training in this regard. It can easily differentiate between family and strangers and thus, any unfamiliar coming in the property will be attacked. If you have friends who visit often, then get the dog acquainted to them one by one, and in the company of a family member. If this is not done, there are very high chances of these people being mauled if your dog sees them entering your property.

5- **Training** a Caucasian Shepherd is easy **if you start at a young age**. The later you start, the more difficult it will be for you to train this dog. This dog needs lots of early socialization so that it can be managed in its adult life. If this dog has not been socialized with people and other animals as a puppy or at a young age, then it can be very difficult to be controlled as an adult.

2. History of the Breed

The Caucasian Shepherd is one of the oldest breeds of dogs in the world. Other common names are Caucasian Ovcharka, Caucasian Mountain Dog and Caucasian Sheep Dog.

They have been raised in the ruthless mountains of the Caucasus, and being the size of a small bear, they have protected flocks of animals, herdsmen and their families for at least 600 years. They have existed not only in the land mass between the Black and Caspian seas but also in Turkey and Iran. But it was most popular in Russia. In Russian it is called "Ovtcharka" which means "sheepdog".

It is the rearing of these dogs in the remotest and most rugged of the mountainous areas of Asia and Europe that have enabled these dogs to evolve into such aggressive and intelligent animals. Natural selection has also enabled only the strongest ones to survive in such austere conditions.

In the 1930s, the Red Star Kennel in Moscow started breeding Caucasian Shepherds for usage in the Red Army as guard dogs. They proved to be better than the German Shepherd when it comes to efficient guarding in the freezing Siberian concentration camps. No wonder they became touted as the pride of Stalin's home country.

These guard dogs started spreading all over Eastern European countries that were occupied by the Soviet Union from Moscow. In 1961, when the Berlin Wall was erected, the DDR utilized the guarding skills of this majestic breed against its own citizens. These robust and ferocious dogs would pounce at anyone trying to cross the border and in a demonic rage, tear apart at the intruder. They would stop at nothing when dealing with trespassers since they have had no human contact while they were being raised. They have no sensation of pain when they are in this trance. But it would instantly become cuddly again when introduced to its acquaintances and family. It is its two-fold behavior and the extent of self sacrifice in guarding its family that makes this breed so majestic and unique.

In 1989, when the Berlin Wall was taken down, 7000 of these dogs were dispersed. They were given new homes throughout Germany.

They are very frequently shown at dog shows throughout Russia and other parts of the former Soviet Union. Extensive breeding programs in Poland, Hungary and Czech and Slovak Republics ensure its popularity remains intact. But its original use as a sheep guardian is declining with time.

The Caucasus Mountains have been inhabited by the oldest living Molosser breed, the Caucasian Shepherd, for many years. There is a huge variety of these types of dogs depending on where they hail from, but a single type has been known to be favored in show rings and literature at the expense of many other variants of the breed. The first appearance of the Caucasian Shepherd outside the Caucasus was in Germany in the 1930s, this particular breed has existed way before that.

3. Description of dogs with different origins

- The Armenian dogs are of two kinds: one is large, has long hair and is often multi-colored; the other is smaller with medium length coat and longer muzzles.
- Daghestan dogs have wide heads, short hair and are multi colored and tall.
- Astrakhan type found in Kabardino-Balkarian region is said to be a cross between the old Georgian and Circassian mountain dog and the Russian show type. Yet the Balkarian Molossers are also rooted in the Sarmatian Mastiff.
- The Turkish Caucasians are divided into four kinds: the Kars Dog, the Garban, the Circassian variant and the Georgian Akhaltsikhe.
- The Garban, which is large, short muzzled and with short hair, mostly red, fawn or brown in colour sometimes with white marks, is extremely vicious. It's a cross between the Kars and the Kangal. Sometimes they hail from crossing the Turkish dogs with the Georgian and Armenian ones.
- The Volkodav sort comes in two kinds: the long haired mountain dog and the short coated steppe dog. They are both smaller than the Armenian and Georgian types and have black masks.
- Mating the dogs from southern Kavkaz with Sage Mazandarani and the Kars, we get the Iranian Sage

Ghafghazi. It is very powerful and lean with a rich coat, called mastiff. It was used as a caravan protector of the Shahsavan nomads who since the 17th century have been breeding this dog. These Iranian Caucasians come in a variety of colors – solid as well as multi.

- There is a rare Kavkaz mastiff that has short-hair and is known as the North-Caucasian Volkodav. It may now get its own breed recognition.

4. Appearance of Caucasian Shepherd Dogs

a. Features

The Caucasian Shepherd has deep set, moderate and dark eyes. The eyes are covered with hairs that provide insulation. Their hips are raised a little from the line of their back, and the tail is covered profusely with heavy haired feathering. Their forelimbs are straight, long and densely boned.

Their paws are heavy and large, with hair between the toes that provide excellent protection and insulation. The black nose is prominent with well opened and large nostrils. The dense coat has heavy feathering and is effective in insulation and weather resistance. The coats of the puppies are finer than those of the adult ones.

b. Colors

The Caucasian Shepherd may be in the following colors:

- White
- Tan
- Brindle
- Pied

- Fawn
- Rust
- Grey
- Cream with a black mask
- Puppies are born black and they lighten gradually.

They may also be available in brown but it is prohibited by the FCI (Fédération Cynologique Internationale, also known as World Canine Organization).

c. Height and Weight
Height: 25-30 inches (64-76cm)

Weight: 80-180 pounds (36-80kg)

d. Life Expectancy
10 – 12 years

Chapter 3. Buying a Caucasian Shepherd Dog

If you are considering buying this dog, there are a few things that you need to be wary of. For starters, like mentioned earlier, this is not a dog for first time owners. You should have had some 'practice' before you go for this breed. It is aggressive and will grow considerably big as it lives. Therefore, be sure of the following questions so you can decide whether or not you are up to handling this breed.

1. Asking for Papers

This is rule number 1. When purchasing dogs, you have the liberty of asking unlimited questions, even to the point of annoying the seller. If living in the US, you are strongly advised only to take AKC papers. This is because AKC enforces its regulations and conducts checks on blood work. So, these are the papers you want to see. The below section will give you an idea what these documents are all about.

The American Kennel Club (AKC)

One of the first things you should notice on an AKC paper is the logo on the top left corner. Their official website also advises that you check out this logo every time you are handed an AKC paper.

Likewise, on the bottom left corner, the paper reads "Limited" and has a box right next to it. If the box to the left is completely darkened, be sure that the dog is not to be used for breeding. However, if the box remains blank, it signifies full registration. That means you can breed your dog and pass on the full papers every time.

There are different companies that make dog papers. Sometimes, you can register a dog just by calling them up and saying *"I'd like to register my dog"* and they say *"Okay"*. There's no checking. But that is not the case with the AKC, so stick with these papers only.

A dog's champion lineage has can be traced through paperwork. You can go back three generations and sometimes more. What you want to know is *"is there a champion in that lineage?"* On AKC paperwork, champion lineage is denoted in red lettering. So if someone tells you they have champion lineage, tell them you want to be sure, and you would like to see the papers.

2. Know the Basics

a. Personality and temperament of the Caucasian Shepherd

This breed is very headstrong and therefore, also requires an owner who is strong in body and mind. The owner should also have time and the self discipline for training and socialization of the dog. These dogs are even tempered and well-balanced, but they are very territorial and will attack strangers right away. They have an inherent trait of recognizing an artificial threat from a real one. They are very protective of their families, property and flock.

They are also very intelligent and self determined. They are not afraid of threats and are independent as well as confident. They will be very loyal once you get acquainted with them and train them. If you are looking for a protection dog who is reliable and agile, then Caucasian Shepherd is the one to get.

When it comes to their level of energy, they are a little phlegmatic. It is a low activity level dog. They have been traditionally bred to keep predators away from their master's flock. Since many of these predators are nocturnal, you will see that the Caucasian Shepherd is more active at night than day.

If you choose to keep your dog outside, know that they bark vehemently when they spot a trespasser. Don't be fooled by them dozing. Even the slightest disturbance will wake them and you will see how quick and agile they are with their attack responses.

b. Age

These dogs need to be familiarized with family members when they are puppies; around 45 days of age. If they are grown and then brought in a family setting, it will be very hard to get them acquainted. Since they are very aggressive, if they are brought in the family at an older age, there are chances that they will attack people. These may include family members also.

c. Gender

As with most breeds, males are larger and more aggressive. Females can be easier to handle because of their smaller size. They are also less dominant and may be easier to handle around children due to their maternal instincts. If you have children in your family, then go for a female one. They are gentler and easier to train but their alertness and guarding traits are as good as a male Caucasian Shepherd. It would be good to discuss this bit with the breeder first. He would ask you things like whether you have owned a dog before or not, and if there are other dogs in your family or not because owning a Caucasian Shepherd has come pre-requisites.

d. Number

The best thing to do would be to start with one puppy and see if you are able to handle this breed. They demand a lot of attention, time, handling and frequent training. Without adequate training, they can get really aggressive with people and other dogs alike. Thus, if you think you can handle more than one such dog and give them all the required care and attention, then go ahead and buy more.

3. How to Ensure You Are Buying a Healthy One?

Caucasian Shepherds can be affected by hip dysplasia and therefore, if you are looking for one, make sure you see their x-rays for signs of the disease. The OFA, or Orthopedic Foundation for Animals issues numbers to dogs that have acceptable hips.

Therefore, whenever you are buying a puppy, look for a breeder that uses x-rayed stock. Make sure you ask for and see the OFA certificates or letters from a certified veterinarian. Breeders with a good reputation will guarantee that their puppies are free from hip dysplasia and other critical genetic defects.

Check that the dog does not have wry legs and a big stomach. Always go for an active puppy that has a good appetite.

a. Shot Records and Vaccinations
Make sure that the puppy is vaccinated. You can confirm this via the International veterinary passport – marks about the kinds and terms of vaccination. Their numbers must coincide and the first three letters should be registered. If the puppy is not vaccinated, then you can lose it the very first day of buying it. Chances of losing the dog to death is 80% if you get it unvaccinated. Although a vaccine cannot completely guarantee you that the dog will not fall ill, it will help avoid a number of dangerous diseases.

Every puppy and every dog should have a shot record, just like your kids do. Every time they receive a shot, there is a sticker right on the bottle that they put on the shot record sheet for future verification.

It's important to know that your dog has been vaccinated as well as de-wormed. When you are selling puppies, you need to keep samples of these shots records on a side note. Get a veterinarian to give shots to your puppy or dog and not yourself to prevent any complications.

b. Dew Claws
For most dog breeds, the dew claws need to be removed when they are still puppies. Dew claws can cause a lot of pain to the

dog throughout their life. So the removal should take place within the first few months of the puppy's life. You can do it yourself. But even asking your veterinarian is not expensive.

4. Questions to ask the breeder

Be sure to ask the following questions from the breeder, shelter or volunteers and staff of a rescue group, when you are buying this breed, or any other for that matter:

Q. What possible health problems might this dog develop?

That's obviously an important question. Only do business with people they know their breed really well. This makes you aware of all the potential hurdles that you may face later on while keeping or even breeding the dog.

Q. How big will the dog get?

Some dogs can be really huge! But you only have a limited area. This is especially true of people who live in apartments. So make sure you know up to what size the dog can grow. Caucasian Shepherds can grow a great big size. You need to do a size approximation before you take the puppy home.

Q. How old will she be before she can reproduce?

This question is of immense importance if you plan to breed the dog. The answer to this question will help you determine when your dog will have puppies, and hence when you will be able to make a profit.

Q. How often will the dog need to be groomed?

Grooming is part of the overall expenditure of keeping a dog, which makes this question highly relevant.

Q. How does she get along with other animals?

In other words, is this a breed that will be fine with other dogs, or do I need to go around with a muzzle on my dog for fear that it might bite other dogs? Although this is signature of any breed, even individual dogs within a breed can act differently.

Q. How long can she be left alone at home?

That's a good question for people who are at work all day. You do not want to come home to a dog that has gone crazy. You don't want ripped-up curtains and couch cushions. If you already have kids who like to jump on the couch and break things, then having a super-energetic dog is simply destructive!

Q. How much exercise does the dog need?

This falls in line with the previous question. Maybe you like to exercise, so you want a dog that can join you.

Q. What are the best training methods for this dog?

You want to know at what age you can begin training your dog. Training makes the ownership experience more pleasant, as the dog knows what you expect from it, i.e. when you want that dog to go to its kennel, etc.

Any honest breeder will answer all of these questions to your satisfaction. In addition, he/she may also give you some breeding advice based on your lifestyle. If the breeder doesn't respond to your inquiries, or doesn't show any interest in dog after it leaves their premises, you may want to look elsewhere.

Some other common questions you can ask the breeder are:

1- What is the energy level of the puppy?
2- How does it act around other animals?
3- How does it respond to visitors, shelter workers and children?
4- What is its personality like?
5- Has it ever hurt or bitten anyone they know about?
6- What is its age?
7- Is it house trained or not?
8- Are there any known health issues with the dog?

5. Where to Buy and For How Much?

The first thing to ensure is that your breeder is a reliable and reputable one. It is cardinal in finding the right puppy. A reputable breeder will always welcome and answer any questions pertaining to the dogs' temperament and health clearances. They will also explain the breed's history and what kind of puppy will make a good pet. Be sure to ask any and all questions pertaining to the dog. Breeders will know their dogs best since they interact with them on a daily basis. They can recommend you the best after taking into account your personality as well as your lifestyle.

a. How do you know which breeder is good?
There are a number of breeders online as well as offline, so how do you tell which is good and which is not? Look out for the following things. They mean trouble.

1- A lot of litters available on the premises
2- Lots of puppies being available at all times
3- Having the puppy of your choice readily available
4- Offering to pay with a credit card online
5- Those who sell puppies without papers at a low price
6- Offering to ship your dog – you will have no control over what you eventually receive

You should look for breeders who actively participate in showing, breeding and training of these dogs. Those belonging to dog clubs can also be deemed reliable. Always ask for references and check back with the older purchasers about the quality of dogs they received. You may have to get on a waiting list to get a healthy dog of your choice.

When looking for a puppy of the Caucasian Shepherd breed, put in as much research as you possibly can. This would be equivalent to researching for a car or any expensive gadget. This dog is hard to train and keep any way, so make sure it doesn't come with any 'pre-purchase faults' that you will have to unnecessarily deal with along with the training and upkeep of this dog. It will save you time, money and a lot of energy in the long run.

b. Where to buy the dog in the US?
When you are searching for your puppy, check out the website of COCA, or **Caucasian Ovcharka Club of America** along with the breed contacts mentioned on the **American Kennel Club's website**. You should choose a breeder who has agreed to abide by the code of ethics of COCA and which calls for the members to work in the cause of reduction of hip dysplasia. They should also sell puppies with a proper guarantee and a sales contract.

If you are looking online, then search up on **Petfinder.com.** They will look up an Ovcharka in your area in a matter of seconds. This website will be very specific in asking your needs, e.g. housetraining status, age, etc or if you want to make a general search, then you can do that too.

AnimalShelter will also help you find animal rescue groups in your area and you can also check out the **'pets looking for homes'** section in the newspaper.

Social media can also come in handy here. Put up a post about you looking for a Caucasian Shepherd. You might just be connected to a seller via the 'Tell 10 to tell 10' sharing principle.

A good idea may be to also talk to local dog experts like dog walkers, vets and groomers. They are well connected to dog owners and if someone is looking to part with their dog or a litter of pups, they usually spread the word via these experts.

Rescue networks like the **Caucasian Ovcharka Club of America** will help you find a perfect companion in the family. Rescue networks are very up front about health issues and they will be great in imparting advice. They may even offer foster opportunities just so you can try how it feels living with a Caucasian Shepherd.

No matter where you get your Caucasian Shepherd dog from, be sure to have a good contract with the seller – be it a rescue group or shelter. The responsibilities of both sides should be spelled out clearly. With **Petfinder**, you get an **Adopter's Bill of Rights**, which will help you understand what is considered normal when buying from a shelter. Some states may have 'puppy lemon laws' and if you happen to buy a dog from one of these states, then make sure that you and the seller both understand your recourses and rights.

Soon after you have adopted the puppy, make sure you take it to a veterinarian. He will identify and diagnose any problems with the dog, and will help you set up a preventive regime which will help you avoid a lot of health issues.

c. How much do they cost in US?

The cost of the dog will depend on whether the dog is imported or bred in the US; whether one or both parents were champions and whether their hips and health are guaranteed. A **pet quality** pup may range from $500 to $1000 or £300 to £600. A **show quality** pup may cost $800 / £480 and up. Imported ones can obviously cost more. Adult or older dogs may be more expensive depending on its quality; whether it has earned any championship points or whether it has had any obedience training.

d. Where to buy the dog in the UK?

You can check out the following websites if you are looking to buy Caucasian Shepherd dogs in the UK:

http://www.caucasian-ovtcharka.co.uk/
http://www.a1caucasians.co.uk/index.html

Apart from the above specific Caucasian Shepherd sellers, there is **pets4homes.co.uk.**

If you are looking for a pre-owned Caucasian Shepherd, then go for preloved.co.uk. You will find a variety of pre-owned dogs that you can choose from.

Apart from websites, just like mentioned in the US market, use social media and dog experts to look for a dog of your choice.

e. How much do they cost in UK?

Again, depending on the age, size, health and parentage, the dog may cost anything between £ 1000 - £ 2000.

6. Registry of a CS

The Caucasian Shepherd is grouped under 'Flock Guard' or 'Guardian' dogs, and they are recognized under FCI, CKC, NKC, ACR, APRI, NAPR, DRA and AKC/FSS.

7. Educate Yourself

The entire process of choosing the right dog to buy requires that you educate yourself about the specific breed you are buying. This holds especially true for a dog like the Caucasian Shepherd. When you have purchased the dogs, you will require a little more extensive research at this stage. You can grab some general educational books, find websites of reputable breeders, books about your specific breed (just like this one!), and you can even join clubs to receive newsletters, emails and other stuff about the breed you have purchased. Search on Google and look for a regular magazine that shares information, tips and tricks about your specific breed.

Searching on the Internet can greatly help you because you can find various websites where you can sell your dogs in the future. Don't forget to bookmark these websites to visit at the right time. These websites can also help you setting up your own website. See the overall set up of the site and its operations. Also focus on the target market and the type of people purchasing dogs. Scale the time period over which they are selling their puppies and most importantly, check out the prices for the different breeds they are asking for.

All this will help you in the future when your pups are ready to be sold. The setup and the pricing strategy will help you get the top dollar for your dogs and in the most efficient manner. If you are still hesitant or skeptical about the whole procedure, realize that if others can do it, you can too. And the biggest attraction is the money you will make with the little effort of owning a beloved pet.

Remember, you do not need a lot of dogs to get started, especially with the Caucasian Shepherd. One would do great and will help you get started more smoothly. Managing a lot of dogs itself could be challenging, so don't get into that in the beginning. However, eventually you can increase the number of dogs you are dealing with for more pups.

Chapter 4. What to Expect Post Purchase

Now that you know any and all aspects and precautions of owning a Caucasian Shepherd Dog, and if you think you meet the criteria of a worthy and suitable owner, then read below for what to expect and do after bringing the dog home.

1. The Adjustment Stage

Now that you have brought the dog home, your first job would be to familiarize the dog with all family members. You can call it acquainting or socializing. The dog has to learn who 'family' is and therefore, who should not be attacked.

Then you need to build a loving bond with the dog. This will help you understand its needs and instincts, and will also enable the dog to have complete trust in you. Then you should begin training the dog. The details of this will be explained later.

The Caucasian can be a house wrecker, so if you are bringing it in, remove all precious and breakable items and invest in a good vacuum cleaner. But like any dog, they too can be trained well. Puppies need to be housebroken and they need to be taught what kind of behavior is permissible and what isn't. Crate training might help a lot, so talk to your breeder about it.

When it comes to shedding, they lose hair all the time but in small quantities. They do, however, 'blow their coat' at least once a year and when that time comes, there are tufts of hair everywhere. Be ready with rakes and combs to get to work. You can minimize this by proper grooming though. This shall also be explained later.

2. Compatibility with co-inhabitants

By co-inhabitants we mean family as well as other pets. The key remains to socialize and acquaint the dog with others in the house.

Caucasians are good with children and would never hurt them on purpose. However, NEVER leave a child alone with the dog. You should ensure that a pecking order is established and that children should not be pushed around. They are large dogs and may not be aware of their own size. This may result in a child being knocked down or stepped on. Therefore, adult supervision is always necessary just like with any other pet. The Caucasian will think of the family as its flock and it will guard them with all its might. Children will be protected from all possible threats, even unfamiliar visitors. Slightly older children with friends should ensure that the dog is not exposed to visiting friends. The friends may like dogs, but your dog might not necessarily return the sentiment.

When it comes to other pets, Caucasians can live with other dogs, cats and livestock for sure. If you have more pets, get a puppy and work on getting them to familiarize with each other and also make them get along. Females may be able to live together more easily; two unneutered male dogs can rarely live peacefully.

3. Lifespan and Size

The life expectancy of the Caucasian Shepherd is 10 – 12 years and during this time they can grow considerably big. They may grow to 24 to 33.5 inches at the shoulder and can weigh up to 160 pounds. Females may be slightly smaller, weighing at more than 80 pounds and a minimum of 24.5 inches.

4. How to Bond with Your Caucasian Shepherd

In order to win the confidence and trust of your Caucasian Shepherd, be sure to build a caring and loving bond with it. When these dogs have a secure knowledge of belonging in a family, they will respond better to their owners' commands, be it for training or for general everyday gestures. As with any relationship, there needs to be mutual respect and trust between you and your dog. Respect is of utmost importance. You need to establish yourself as the alpha male. If respect is not there, then it is impossible building a relationship with your dog.

In order to build a strong bond with your Caucasian Shepherd, do the following:

1- Spend quality time with the dog
2- Experience life with the dog by being with it in the world; do not keep it isolated and stranded in the house
3- Promote mutual respect and love
4- Make an effort to understand the dog's needs and find ways to communicate with it.

5. Pros and Cons of Owning a Caucasian Shepherd

Pros:

1- It is the best dog when it comes to protection. No other dog will protect your family and property like this one will.
2- They love to work. Give them a job and they will be happy. That job can be protection, a walk in the neighborhood (their equivalent of a patrol) or even fetching.
3- Because of the above, they are easy to train.
4- They are easily housebroken and since they are highly intelligent, they can learn meanings of new words on their own.
5- They are highly loyal to family and demand love. They are marshmallows in front of family members and will shower you with unconditional love. They will mope when a fellow canine has moved from the vicinity and might not even eat for days if a coveted bitch has left the neighborhood.

Cons:

1- This dog is not for everyone, especially not amateur owners. This is because they are big and need excellent training in how to behave.

2- If you are very social and have friends frequently over, then this dog isn't for you. It will attack all intruders and you don't want to lose your friends that way.

3- You cannot let the dog just be on its own. It has to be under constant supervision of an experienced handler. The point is not to malign the dog here, but outlining the fact that this dog's mission is to protect and defend, and it only resorts to violence when it sees a threat. You do not want innocent strangers being mauled by this dog and therefore they need supervision.

4- Those who do not know about this breed and who try to play with it may get attacked. Hence, if you live in a community, then you cannot be sure who is aware of this kind of dog, and who isn't. Even if the dog sees the family teenager in a tussle with another teenager, it will attack the latter. It will not even be the dog's fault. It is just doing what it has been bred and trained to do.

5- They will bark every time they feel threatened or if they hear a sound in the vicinity. Thus, if you live in a condominium, a townhouse or even a housing society, then this dog will prove to be a menace with all its barking.

Chapter 5. How To Take Care of A Caucasian Shepherd

This dog needs a lot of handling and care. It can be pertaining to its grooming and training, and it is a continuous process, and not something you can do once a week. So make sure you allocate a certain amount of time for this breed in your schedule.

1. Grooming

How your dog looks can influence how it feels and also the way you perceive or treat it. There have been cases wherein a Caucasian's behavior has changed due to lack of grooming, cleaning and care.

Proper grooming is necessary because it will not only make your dog look good but will also develop its self esteem, and you can always flaunt your stunning dog in front of others when you feel like it.

a. Coat

The Caucasian Shepherd has a double coat that comprises of a topcoat and an undercoat. The outer coat has long and coarse hair while the undercoat is fine and soft. If the outer coat is soft or wavy, then it is not normal. The length of the coat can be short, medium or long. Those with a long coat have a mane that surrounds the neck and the hind legs and tail have extensive feathering which give a fluffy and thick look. Those dogs that have medium length coats do not have much of a mane and the feathering is also scant on the rest of the body. The ones with a short coat have no feathering or mane, and these dogs are very rare.

b. Proper way of Brushing

In order to keep the Caucasian's double coat healthy, you need to brush him thoroughly at least twice a week. Brushing improves blood circulation, makes the coat shiny and healthy and helps you bond with the dog.

There is a proper way of brushing your Caucasian Shepherd dog and it involves the following steps:

1- In the beginning, brush in the opposite direction of hair growth, first with a slicker bush and later with a wide-toothed or medium comb. The slicker brush removes all loose hair and the comb will help with the untangling.
2- Next, brush in the direction of the hair growth and attempt to reach its skin as you brush.
3- Then, with a flea comb, remove the fleas and any tangles that were left behind. You should first part the coat and comb by starting from the root up.
4- If the dog has hairy paw pads, use electric clippers to clip them. Do not remove the hair in between the pads and clip only the excess hair.

Proper brushing will not also prevent matting, which can be a painful experience. Even if mats and tangles do form, use a detangle solution and a medium - toothed comb.

The dog will 'blow coat' annually, which means that it will undergo a heavy shed. When this happens, make sure you give the dog warm baths and frequent brushing to help him shed the coat faster. This will also curtail the amount of hair that will fall on your furniture, carpet, floor and clothing.

Any other requirement is routine care just like for all dogs: trim its nails and clean its ears regularly.

c. Dew Claws

A dew claw is the nail that sits up on the front two paws of a dog. There is a history behind it. The dew claw is actually used by dogs for holding food or bones between their paws while they eat. Nowadays, dogs wear collars; they have blankets, and even their own beds. Plus, they are moving in and out of fences.

So if your dog puts his paws through fences, engages them in any activity (such as digging), or uses them to hold an object, these dewclaws will catch and tear off. This can be painful for a dog, which is why they have to be removed early on.

Why Do It?

Removing dew claws is not necessary. But it does give more value if you are a breeder, and also to the puppies. It's the same as say a circumcision of a child. It is done when they are young when it is not so painful, but it prevents many problems that may arise later on.

The Procedure for Removal

With a pair of scissors and some triple ointment antibiotic, you can do this yourself; it's really not hard at all. If you decide to take them to a vet and if you are a breeder, let them know you are one beforehand. You may be able to get a discount. You can get up to a 25% discount because they know you will be bringing a lot of puppies later on.

Prevention is better than cure

If you have a car and you are constantly changing the oil and fluids, then you don't have to deal with drastic repairs over time. Thus, you save thousands of dollars down the road.

The same is true with puppies. With dogs, the slightest negligence can get real expensive.

d. Nail Trimming:

Dogs and their owners both hate trimming nails of the dog. Dogs do not like sharing their paws and if the nails are cut too short, it is too painful for them. Owners are nervous while doing this because they are afraid they will hurt their dog. The dog will also become averse to nail trimming if you hurt it once in the process. Thus, it is important to learn the right way to trim nails before hand, and then exercise high caution when you actually do it. Most dogs need nail trimming once a month while others may need more or less depending on the rate of their nail growth. A substitute to trimming nails is the use of a rotary tool to file down the nails.

When you are cutting your dog's nails, do it at a place where it will be comfortable. You should ideally have another person with you to hold the dog still.

Once comfortably seated, grab the paw, but don't squeeze it. Hold the trimmers with your hand, place your thumb on bottom of the foot pad; line your trimmer by placing the blade where you will eventually cut. This will tell you where you will make the cut. Squeeze the trimmer in one swift motion and avoid cutting if the dog is moving. The best part of the nail to cut is 2-3 mm away from the pink area. If they are dark colored nails, cut little at a time until you see fleshy white or gray area under. This is where the flesh starts and you do not want to cut that.

e. Ear Care:

Your dog can store a copious amount of yeast and bacteria in its ears if not cleaned properly. You can clean the ears after their monthly bath if its normal. In case of chronic ear disease, multiple cleanings in a day may be required. For proper cleaning of your dog's ears, you will need an ear cleansing solution, cotton balls, cotton tip applicators, tweezers and a towel.

First hold the ear flap up and squirt some cleaner in it near the opening. Then, massage the base of the ear if it shakes its head. If the ears are very dirty, let the dog shake itself. This will loosen up the debris inside. After the shake, clean the ear with a cotton ball or gauze, and your finger by wiping it. Applicators may also be used for this part. Do not force it further than you can see as the eardrum may be damaged.

f. Bathing:

Most dogs need a monthly bath but bathing more frequently is not harmful. Use a soap-free shampoo that is made for dogs. The vet may recommend a shampoo suitable for the dog and its skin. You will also need soft towels, brushes and combs, an apron for yourself and a bath mat to prevent slipping.

First wet your dog completely. Remember to check the temperature of the water first. Apply shampoo everywhere except eyes, face and genital area. Make lather. Mix two parts shampoo with one part water for application. Rub, scrub and massage your dog for several minutes. Remember to clean the feet thoroughly. A rubber tool with nubs can also be used to bathe a dog. Then rinse out all the shampoo avoiding the eyes but covering the crevices. Then let your dog shake a little and then towel-dry excess water. You can try blow-drying also if your dog allows it.

You can do all of this grooming yourself at home, or go to a professional dog groomer in your area to get this done. There are many who do this professionally at reasonable costs.

2. Tail Docking

Some people look for cut tails. But cut tails look good on certain breeds. Once again, you can learn to do it on your own or have a vet do it for you.

3. Worming

Almost all dogs are infested with parasites of some kind or the other. Most dogs develop immunity that keeps the population of parasites in check. However, under conditions of ill health or stress, this strength can break down. In such a case, there is a risk that worms will increase in number and will eventually produce signs of intestinal infections and will result in anemia, weight loss, diarrhea and blood in the feces.

Worms are very common for dogs and if you want them to be in perfect health, you need to take all the important measures to keep them safe. Worming is a subject I want to get into directly because it is very difficult for dogs to be able to prevent all types of worms, including tape worms and heart worms that dogs are vulnerable to.

Usually, they get it from the yard, eating mice or fleas, or gross food. Obviously, you cannot watch out for everything at all times because you never know what a dog is going to get into. Therefore, preventative measures are best in this case.

The next thing you need to ponder over is the types of worms that your dog might have and the right treatment to get rid of them. You need to schedule a time for the dog and de-worm him/her. Do not treat on a temporary basis. Behave as if your dog has worms all the time. The best thing about worming medication that will not turn you off is that you can get a whole lot of it without spending a lot of money. If you regularly find worms on your dog, you can treat them constantly. In short, you need to de-worm your dog for all types of worms.

If you have a female dog, the ideal time to de-worm her is before she has puppies. This will ensure that the puppies will be free of worms when they are born. Worms can be fatal for puppies. What I am trying to say here is that adult dogs have stronger immunity to fight of worms as well as bear worming medication multiple times in a year, i.e. before a dog is bred, while she is in heat and ready to have pups, and even while she is pregnant. However, you need to make sure you have the right de-worming medication that suits her specific condition.

One of the best medications when they are pregnant is Fenbendazole. It is also called Safe-Guard. This is a worm prevention medicine. It is safe and can be given to your dog constantly while she is pregnant. In fact, you can even give this one to puppies if you suspect that they might have worms. It is a safe de-worming medication that does not cause allergies or any other problems to dogs that can be cause by other stronger doses of de-worming medication. This medicine is tried and tested and therefore highly recommended.

As far as dosage is concerned, you need to be a little careful. The medication comes in a large bottle and is usually available for cattle, sheep, lambs, goats and horses. Thus, the dosage prescribed is also according to a larger scale. For dogs, keep the dosage to 1cc per 10 pounds of dog. Give one dosage per day for three consecutive days. Then give the next dosage after 14 days following the same cycle. You may want to do additional research according to the specific breed you have. For any confusion, feel free to call the veterinarian and talk to them about it.

So this is the way medication should be provided to dogs to free them from all types of worms, except for the tapeworm. You can witness these worms if your dog has them because they can be seen with the naked eye. They are usually present on the skin and near the butt area of the dog. Choose a dose that is specifically for treating tapeworms. You do not need to use it regularly. A single dose is enough. Check to see if you find more tapeworms and use only when you are sure your dog has them.

Where to Buy

Where to buy is a very important question when it comes to buying medication supplies for your dogs or any other pet products. Researching online is the key to follow here. Be specific about the breed when you research and follow people's recommendations because they are usually tried and tested. When you research online, there are almost countless places you will find for the products you are searching for, thus it is very important that you compare prices, follow reviews and go only for the best available in the market. If you are searching offline, ask your friends and acquaintances with pets, where they get their stuff from.

4. Feeding

Just as for any living being, the correct diet and submission of food to a Caucasian Shepherd dog are essential for the health of your puppy. If you feed your puppy insufficiently, and are not careful with its upkeep, then dry or tender constitution may form, which is absolutely not good. Similarly, overfeeding or abundant feeding may result in friability and dampness in the constitution.

a. Types of Diets for Dogs

Let's look at the types of diets for dogs. We will talk specifically about feeding the Caucasian Shepherd too later on.

As human diets vary, the list of foods that dogs can eat is quite extensive.

Dry Food Diet

First there is a dry food diet. This is the most common diet among dogs, and it actually helps in cleaning their teeth. Not to mention, they are also getting the necessary nutrients. The problem with wet foods is that they have a lot of salts and sugars, which is not all healthy for the canine.

Raw Food

Next, we move into raw food. There are a lot of companies that offer raw food diet for dogs. And they will deliver super healthy foods to your door, like meats, vegetables and ground up bones. Although the raw food diet is healthy, it can prove to be expensive in the long run.

Dry food diets are now what I consider to be the best for your dog. So I will show some of the ways to feed your dog that are hassle free and don't take much time.

Along with the types of dog foods, you should also be aware of food allergies. The problem with food allergies in dogs is that the warning signs are not the same as with humans. When we have an allergy, our eyes swell up and the nose gets stuffy. But this doesn't happen with dogs.

So the signs you should watch out are as follows:

- Their face gets itchy
- They'll rub inside their mouth because their teeth itch.
- Your dog can become overweight and even incur heart problems
- Their fur can thin out, and the skin flakes off easily as well.

Sometimes you treat these conditions by simply by changing their diet. However, changing the diet does affect your dog's intestinal system. So any transition should be gradual.

You should also know some of the foods that cause allergies in dogs. Soy, beef, pork, chicken, milk, and corn are common items in this list. Safe items include lamb, rabbit, and rice. They have to be mixed in foods, and you'll notice some of their symptoms start to go away as the dog adapts to this diet.

b. The Caucasian Shepherd's Diet
Despite of the dog's adaptability with humans, its diet remains that of its ancestors because of the nature and function of its digestive organs. The dog is used to having porridge or sweets, or any of their likes. Meat is necessary – in raw form. A balanced

diet for this dog must consist of fats, carbohydrates, proteins, mineral substances, vitamins and trace elements.

The dog can be picky about eating in the hot summer months. Make sure you give them fresh food in the summer, since food gets perished faster then. Heat may cause a loss of appetite due to confusion in the autonomic nervous system via temperature change or lack of certain nutrients.

In the winters, be very careful about their diet, since there is a high likelihood of them getting obese.

c. What to Feed At 3 months:
The puppy at 3 months should be fed one egg a day and after 3 months, 2 eggs a day.

You can also give them fish after 3 months of age but since its nutritional value is lower, its amount should be doubled. Remove the head, and pass the raw meat with bones through a meat grinder. Feed this to the puppy. If it's a river fish, give it only in boiled form.

Prior to 1.5 months of age, the dog should only be given force meat and not pieces, in order to avoid indigestion.

Fats should be given in a limited quantity because it can lead to indigestion and disruption of liver activity.

Milk should be given to puppies and feeding bitches, fresh and in small quantities.

Check out the table below for feeding guidance for a puppy of 1-1.5 months in the **traditional manner**:

1st feeding	6:00 - milk porridge of buckwheat or rice grouts + 0.5 tsp of creamy oil
2nd feeding	9:00 - cottage cheese + 1tsp of wiped black currant
3rd feeding	12:00 - soup (cabbage soup) + boiled meat
4th feeding	15:00 - kefir or sour milk
5th feeding	18:0 - stewed vegetables + meat
6th feeding	21:00 - milk porridge + oil + half an egg
7th feeding	00:00 - meat stuffing (carrot or beet in small pieces) + sour cream

Check below for more information on feeding your puppy:

Age	Quantity of feedings during the day	Approximate volume of each feeding
1-2 months	7	100 - 120gr
2 - 3 months	6	150 - 220gr
3 - 4 months	5	250 - 450gr
4 - 8 months	4	500 - 800gr
8 - 17 months	3	800 - 1200gr
From 1,5 years	2	1,5 - 2,1 kg

The food must have a porridge-like consistency and should have some salt added. Always give water in a separate dish to the dog. The puppies should be fed frequently and with small portions. Large meals can disrupt development, formation of the backbone and deflection of the back and limbs.

The food basin should be level with elbow joint of the dog, and should be offered to the dog for 15 minutes. If the dog doesn't eat it, remove the basin. In the next feeding, decrease the portion size so that the dog doesn't overeat.

Check out the below table for feeding your puppy in the contemporary way:

47

1st feeding	7:00 - dry fodder ("Royal Canin", for the puppies of large breeds); well soaked in water for 3-4 hours and watered with 10% fresh cream
2nd feeding	12:00 - stuffing of raw meat (beef or entrails scar)
3rd feeding	17:00 - dry fodder, soaked in water
4th feeding	Stuffing of raw or boiled meat

d. Feeding an adult dog:

Adult dogs are better fed entrails or meat. Entrails are cheaper and less wasteful. You can even use general dog feed brands available in the supermarket.

Provision of vitamins and minerals is also necessary for the dogs, so please consult the veterinarian for the dosage your particular dog requires.

e. Gravity Fed Feeders

Gravity fed feeders are nice because they allow you to put the dry food in a container that your dog can consume for a whole week. This saves you a lot of time and energy. Also, if you are out of the house, your dog still gets food and water.

f. Pro Plan

Pro Plan is a brand of dog food made from lamb and rice formula. I am not promoting it, but it is a trusted brand world over, but there many other brands of dog foods that have similar effects. The benefit of using Pro Plan is that every time you buy a bag, there are points that you can cut out and receive discounts. They also give you free food when your dog has puppies. You just have to subscribe to Pro Plan on their site.

g. Foods to Avoid
Cooked Bones

No matter what the legend holds, do not feed your dog cooked bones. They can result in their teeth being ground off, injuries and internal diseases being caused, hemorrhages, rectum diseases and bolts.

If you are eating Kentucky Fried Chicken, you don't want to give those cooked bones to your dog. The reason is that these dry out and break into small pieces easily that will get stuck in your dog's tummy or throat. This can cause infection. You can give them raw bones all you like.

Raw Hides

Then there are raw hides. If you ever go into a pet store, they have all of these parts of animals you can feed your dog, including bones, rawhides, pig ears, feet and snouts. All of these are just leftovers that are now being sold.

You can give these to your dog, but make sure you are getting the right size. You want to make sure you are not giving a small chunk of rawhide to a big dog because they are going to break pieces off and these can get caught in their digestive tract. So when you first give a rawhide or pig ear or snout to a dog it's really healthy for them, but just make sure you are watching them so they won't choke.

Chocolate

Moving on, you always hear that chocolate is poisonous for dogs. In small amounts, it can be OK. It will take a lot of chocolate to poison a dog but over a long period of time it is poisonous to a dog. So an occasional cake treat should not freak you out!

h. Dog Treats

If you want to feed your dog treats, they are many very cool websites on the Internet that teach you how to make them on your own. These are really healthy and give you a hand while training your pet. Treats reinforce good behavior and they are enjoyable to them because of the sugar content.

Below are some treat ideas for your dog:

- Beef jerky
- Popcorn
- Meat baby food
- Ice cubes
- Cubed lunch meat
- Dried liver
- Shredded cheese
- Cream cheese, Easy Cheese or peanut butter– just a lick!
- Cereal
- Kibble
- Carrot or apple pieces

Make sure they are pea-sized and easily accessible. Give it a mix of treats so it does not know what is coming next.

5. Accommodation

Usually a dog that stays inside the house has all its needs met. It can stay cool when it's hot outside in the summer and will stay warm when it's cold outside in the winter. But the dog that stays outside needs protection.

Doggies Doors

There are many types of doggy doors to choose from. You can put them in walls or in sliding glass doors. Some varieties can even be cut into your main door. These doggie doors allow you to bring the dog inside the house or keep him out easily, depending on the situation.

Outside Care

If your dog always remains outside, you need appropriate fencing, a dog house, heating pads, and heating lamps. If there are wires outside your house, these also need to be protected from chewing.

Secure fencing is necessary for not only keeping your dog from running away, but also from avoiding other dogs coming in. If you have a female dog in heat, other dogs in the neighborhood will become professional acrobats, so you want to protect your females from being bred by another breed you aren't sure about, and that too without papers.

As far as dog houses are concerned, these come in different designs and you can build your own as well. But make sure that the dog house should not be larger than three times your dog's body size. Also keep a small opening. This will help the dog to stay warm.

Additionally you can cut a hole in the dog house and add a heat lamp. You can see from inside your house that your dog is warm because the light is on.

Finally, you should go to dog farms and dog supply companies and see what they have. The large dog stores also have a lot of things that come in handy when you want to keep your dog safe and healthy.

Also, please be wary of the following pointers when planning accommodation for your dog:

1- The dog should get proper sun light since it helps with the metabolism, increases the dog's vitality, helps relinquish bad bacteria and hence, many diseases. But too much heat can also result in overheating the dog and its eventual sun stroke or thermal stroke.

2- Coarse and loamy soil is favorable to animals since they leak air and water, and get dry quickly after rain. Fine grained soil retains water and air, and can always remain wet which can be unfavorable to dogs.

3- Do not keep the puppy near heating machines, near the kitchen, bathroom, in the hall near the doors or in a draughty place.

4- The floor where the dog stays should be clean and the bedding should always be clean and shaken up for the comfort of the dog. You can use a child's old mattress for the dog, but wash the bedding at least twice a month.

5- Never lock the puppy or dog in a dark room or where movement is restricted. Otherwise it can result in rachitis and joint weakness along with overall underdevelopment.

6- Never tie the puppy – the leash can result in a soft back and irregular limbs.

7- Discourage the puppy from leaning under low furniture since it can deform the back.

8- Refrain from handing over the puppy to children, as there is a danger of them dropping it.

9- Do not leave the puppy alone for too long as they get really sad and frequent aloofness can result in fault in the character when the dog grows up.

10- Do not pull out anything from the puppy's teeth since that can break its teeth and damage its bite. Carefully unclamp the mouth and remove whatever was bothering it.

11- You can teach the puppy how to swim at 3 months of age. Never throw it in the pool. Take its toy into the pool and then usher him in. When it's done, take it out of the pool and let it run around so it can dry itself off.

6. Setting the Rules

As soon as you bring in the dog in your house, make sure you dominate yourself as the 'alpha' figure, and that it needs to listen to you. It needs to know that you are the leader of the pack and therefore, in charge. You need to set the rules from the beginning and follow them every single time. If you let the rules down even once, the dog will take you for granted. Just watch how a bitch lays down the rules. She never lets the offspring dominate her even though the litter is kind of big, unlike many humans. If a bone is hers, she will take it. If a puppy tries to snatch it, it will soon learn a lesson – the hard way.

Follow the below guidelines in order to establish yourself as the 'alpha' figure:

1- Come in or go out through the door first – you are the leader, so you should lead, always.
2- Eat first. Feed your dog after you have finished eating
3- If the dog is lying in your way, make it move out of the way instead of circling around it.
4- Do not let him set the rules. Give it attention only when you think it is required and not every time it demands.
5- Never let it sleep with you in your bed. Mark its sleeping area clearly so it remembers.

Once your 'alpha' status is established, it will be very easy to train your dog. But if you fail here, all your training efforts will go in vain.

7. Transporting

It would always be best to transport your new or old pet in your own car. Many people get uncomfortable around dogs, especially one of this size. Therefore, avoid using public transport although it might not always be prohibited. Caucasian Shepherds are highly territorial, easily aroused by strangers and even a slight nudge to its master in a crowded place may tick it off.

Dogs are generally prohibited entry in shops, restaurants, malls, and some beaches. There will always be signs depicting prohibition of bringing in the pet. Just follow those and you should be fine.

8. Possible Illnesses and Plan of Action

Like all dogs, even Caucasian Shepherds are susceptible to certain common health problems. These problems can be caused by parasites like fleas, dog ticks, puppy worms like roundworms, tapeworms and heartworms.

They may also be prone to elbow and hip dysplasia, heart problems and obesity.

You should visit a dog breeder to learn how to identify dog health problems and how to best tackle them.

9. Training

The Caucasian Shepherd is an intelligent breed but it needs to be trained otherwise an uncontrollable and untamed Caucasian can be very dangerous.

While training this breed, you will find that it is very stubborn and reluctant to learn; it will also not respond to humans, toys, or food a lot of times, but the key is to be patient and to be in control at all times. You must always use positive reinforcement to train this breed because they are intrinsically a proud breed and will not respond very well to being threatened or physically abused. Having said that, some Caucasian Shepherd are more easy to train than others, it will all depend on the dog's character.

If you have bought a puppy, and once it is old enough, a 'Puppy Kindergarten' is highly recommended. You can contact a local breed or obedience club in order to find one). This should be followed by a basic obedience class.

The dog will voluntarily assume that it is the alpha figure, and this needs to be rectified. All human members of the family must be treated above the dog in the status of the pack. We have already mentioned how to establish 'alpha' role in your relationship with the dog, so please follow it at all times.

Before you begin training your dog, it is important that you bond with it first. We had shown you how to go about it earlier on. Once you have established that bond with your Caucasian Shepherd, then make note of the following phases you will encounter while training your dog.

You can see a dog in professional training class on the next picture, where a dog is being trained to protect a property.

a. Phases of Dog Training

The Teaching Phase: In this phase, you will have to physically demonstrate to the dog what you want him to do.

The Practicing Phase: Make your dog practice what you have taught it again and again. This will make it perfect in all of the endeavors it opts for, and will also learn faster.

The Generalizing Phase: You need to practice with your dog at different locations and in an environment that has few distractions. These places can include the park, on the street when you are walking him, etc. Command him and have him practice what you have taught it. Practicing in different locations with lesser distractions will help the dog learn faster and retain the lessons in a much better way.

The Testing Phase: If and when you think you have achieved 90% success with your dog in its training and you will know this when it responds to most of your commands, then it is time to up your game. Start testing the dog and its accuracy in newer locations and with more distractions. An example of such a place is your local mall. Take your dog there and command him to do one of things you taught it. The response may not come right away, but do not lose hope. Try again until you see the response you have been looking for. The whole idea is to acclimatize the dog to an environment that is new to it. It must know that it has to obey you at all times, and everywhere. Use the 3 Ps while testing and training your dog: patience, perseverance and praise.

Internalizing Phase: This is the most rewarding phase in which your dog does everything without you having to command it to do so. You need to be wary of the following:

- Do not scold your dog if he fails to obey a command. It is not his fault that you are a lousy trainer.
- You need to be patient and persistent before you see some results with your dog.
- Always appreciate and praise your dog when it does something right. A little encouragement will go a long way when it comes to your Caucasian Shepherd.

b. Teaching tricks to your dog

Dogs are intelligent. They are keen learners and love to please their owners. Most of them are easy to train and can be taught a few basic and some advanced tricks using positive reinforcement techniques.

The Caucasian Shepherd is not a typical dog that likes to play fetch although I do know some people who's dog does like playing it. It all depends on your dog's character! I have listed these tricks anyway, in case your dog will love doing tricks.

In order to train your dog, make sure you have some tools handy to facilitate the process. It is recommended that you use a bag of training treats. These are called primary 'reinforcers' and are to be given to the dog as a reward with every command. Below are some tricks and their methods of training your dog to perform them:

Shaking Hands

It would be such a delight if your dog shakes hands with all your friends at your command. It will be praised for being friendly and you will be lauded for being such a good teacher.

Teaching your dog the 'shaking hands' trick needs patience. First, your dog should be trained to sit on its hind legs. If it has already learnt that and is in sitting position, pick your dogs paw and shake it physically while saying 'shake' and immediately give it a treat to eat.

Repeat this procedure seven to eight times, treating the dog at every shake and praising it continuously. Your dog will soon learn the trick and then offer its paw to shake whenever you call out the command.

High Five

For this trick, your dog needs to know the 'shaking hands' trick. Tell your dog to shake hands but keep your palm up in the air for it to reach it. If your dog does not reach up to your palm, just shake it and physically lift its paw up.

Try doing this three to four times. When your dog understands where to give you his paw, change the command to 'high five' and feed it a treat for every correct move. Also, praise it by saying 'good job' time and again to keep it motivated.

This is a pretty simple trick if your dog has learned to respond to the 'shake hands' trick well. Your dog will not take much time learning this clever move and you can do a 'high five' with it the next time you are sitting at a football game with your friends.

Wave

For this trick, your dog first needs to learn the 'shaking hands' trick properly. When you are sure your dog will respond to the 'shake' command, only then proceed with teaching the 'wave' trick.

Extend your hand in front of your dog as if to shake. Call out 'shake' for it to lift its paw from the ground. When the dog lifts its paw, do not accept it but keep moving your hand higher so that it continues to reach for it. Call out 'wave' and give it a treat at that moment.

Repeat this step as many times as necessary until your dog learns the trick. Accompany the lesson with repeated petting. Also, praise your dog with words like 'good boy' or 'good girl'.

You can ask your dog to wave at your friends or neighbors to test his response. Keep treats with you when you go out for a walk with your dog. Continuously practice the command with it and keep treating and praising it for his response.

Play Dead

Before teaching your dog this trick, make sure it has been physically active for five to ten minutes. It should be ready to relax after the workout. Also, your dog should have learnt the 'down' command before teaching it this trick.

When your dog is a little exhausted, use the 'down' command to make it sit. After your dog leans onto one side, gently push it over on the side it was leaning on saying 'play dead'. When he is lying on its side, praise your dog and give it a treat.

You can also give your dog a tummy scratch to make it happy. Repeat this trick as many times as necessary until your dog learns to obey your command without you having to use any pressure to roll it over on its side.

Fetch

Teaching your dog the 'fetch' trick is a great way to develop a strong bond with your pet. You can play with your dog and at the same time, the game is a good workout for it.

Usually dogs love chasing balls but if your pet is a little reluctant, you can guide it a little to perform the trick. Take a small ball that your dog can easily hold in its mouth and throw it a little away from the dog. Then call out 'fetch' for your dog to go after it. If your dog does not make any moves to go after the ball, go and pick it up yourself and treat it.

You can also slit the ball and fill it with a few treats. Your dog will surely go after a treat-filled ball and will bring it back to you to get the treat.

Soon, your dog will learn to go after the ball itself. When it returns, do not take the ball away from it immediately. It may not be willing to give it to you. Instead bribe it with a treat to drop the ball. After a few attempts, try this trick with other things like a stick or dowel to avoid it getting too attached to the ball.

Roll Over

Ensure that your dog has already learnt the 'play dead' trick before teaching it this one. After your dog is lying on its side, use a treat to lure it. Move your hand above the dog's head and round to the other side. Your dog should turn his neck and body to follow the treat. You should say 'roll over' to get your dog accustomed to the command. Also, keep praising and petting your dog throughout the exercise. Make sure the dog gets up on his four legs after each roll.

An alternate method to teach this trick is to use gentle pressure. When your dog is lying on its side, gently hold the front and hind legs of your dog with both hands and pull them over to the other side, completely turning it over. Keep repeating the command and praising your dog to let it know what you want it to do.

It is important to not force your dog to do anything. If your dog does not like you holding its legs, you better leave them without a struggle. When teaching the trick, roll your dog on soft surfaces like grass or a carpet so that it does not hurt its back.

Bow

To teach this trick, you have to keep an eye on your dog when he wakes up from his sleep. As soon as he stretches, say 'take a bow' and give it a treat. Say that every time your dog takes a big stretch. In a few weeks, your dog will automatically take a bow or stretch for you when you tell it to.

An alternate method to teach this trick is to keep a treat on the ground under your pet's nose and let it take it by bending down. Ensure that the dog does not completely go down on the floor. If he does that, keep your hand under his belly while treating it and saying 'take a bow'. This method may later lead the dog to only take a bow when he sees a treat.

Speak

This is a fun trick and will help you take control of your dog's bark when you take it out for a walk. First, try finding out what makes your dog bark. Every dog is different and may bark at different things. If your dog barks at the ringing telephone, call out 'speak' whenever the phone rings.

By repeating this a couple of times, your pet will learn to bark when you tell it to. Treat and praise your pet as often as you can. Gradually, stop using the telephone ring and try testing it to speak without it.

You can also teach your dog to be quiet after teaching it to speak. After making your dog speak, stand in front of it and say 'quiet' or 'shh' while he is barking. As soon as he stops barking, give it a treat and pet it. This will allow you to keep your dog under control when you are outside.

Kiss

What's better than getting affection in return from your pet? Most dogs will instinctively lick your cheeks if you pet them. If your dog does not respond to affection or if you want your dog to only lick your cheek on command, then you can teach it the 'kiss' trick.

Put a little peanut butter on your cheek or hold a treat to your cheek with your finger and say, "Give me a kiss." Your dog will come running to lick your cheek. Rub his ears and pet it for a job well done. Practice this with your dog a few more times and then try doing the trick without using the treat.

You can also make your dog a lady-charmer by teaching it to kiss the hand on command. Make sure your dog is able to differentiate between your hand and your cheek. Once your dog has learnt the trick, you can test your dog in your social circle. Your dog will certainly become the centre of attention and will be showered with kisses in return.

Stand

This is a cool trick to show off to your friends. Just make your dog sit in one place. Hold a treat above it and let it reach for it. When the dog stands on its hind legs, say 'stand' and keep moving the treat so he walks on his hind legs a little. Praise and treat it for a good job by saying 'good boy' or 'good girl'.

When your dog has learnt the trick, try making it stand by just wiggling your fingers on top of his head. Praise and pet your dog when it tries to take little steps. This will encourage it to do a better job every time you tell it to stand.

Making it stand only with the treat is not a good idea, as then your dog may not stand at the command, but only when it sees the treat.

Cross Your Paws

This trick works well if you want to show your family and friends what a sophisticated dog you have. The 'cross your paws' trick is quite advance and your dog may take some days to learn it. Initially, wear a protector on your hand as your dog might scratch it while learning the trick. Make your dog sit down on all fours and then take a treat in our hand but do not give it to it. Your dog will try to take it out of your hand by using its mouth but after a few attempts will use its paw. When your dog learns to put its paw on your hand to get the treat, praise and treat your dog.

Next, offer your hand to your dog and while he tries to paw at it, move your hand onto its other paw. Initially, your dog may move the other paw too but soon it will learn to keep one paw still while moving the other paw onto the still paw. You can say 'cross your paws' and offer it ample of praise. Rub his ears and say 'good dog' to encourage it to perfect his actions. Very soon your dog will be crossing its paws without the treat, just on your verbal command.

You can make your dog sit in public with you with crossed paws and let passersby admire your refined and sophisticated pet.

Spin

The activity of training your dog becomes interesting and fun with every trick. You can teach your dog to spin in a whole circle with the 'spin' trick. To teach the trick, you need to hold out a treat for your dog to see. Make sure not to give it to it yet. Once he attempts to get the treat, just move it in a circle in front of your dog while saying 'spin'. Your dog will follow your hand and complete a rotation. This calls for some praise and petting. Continuous practice with this trick will soon make your dog understand what he is required to do when you call out the spin command.

You can also teach your dog to go the other way round. You can change your commands and call out 'spin right' or 'spin left' for your dog to spin each way. Do not make your dog over spin. Making it do more than two rotations will make it dizzy.

Which One?

This trick will train your dog to pick out which hand of yours holds the treat. Just take a treat in one hand and then close both fists. Put your fists in front of your dog and ask it 'which one?' Your dog will pry initially with its mouth at your fists. Do not open your hands. Wait long enough for the dog to use his paws instead of his mouth. When he learns to use his paws to point to the correct hand, treat and pet it generously. Be sure to wear a protector to avoid getting scratched by your dog.

You can show off this trick to friends who will be amazed at your dog's intelligence. If your dog does not use his paws and continues to pry with his mouth at the correct hand, let it do it. Your friends will still be awestruck by this wonderful trick.

Hide

This is a really cute trick to teach your dog. Your friends will simply adore it after watching it perform the 'hide' trick. To teach your dog the trick, you need a spray bottle with some water in it. Gently spray a light mist of water onto your dog's face while saying 'hide'. Your dog may respond in many ways. It may try to drink the water, shake its head, run away or hide his eyes with his paw.

To get your dog to hide his eyes, try spraying gently onto his eyes. When he hides his eyes with his paw, give it a treat and praise it. The encouragement will build confidence in your dog. You can then practice this step a few times until you only use the spray bottle and your dog follows your command without the water being sprayed on its face. Stop using the bottle completely after a few more practice sessions. Your dog will soon learn to follow your order when you just use your hands to make the spraying motion and verbally order your dog to hide.

If your dog does not like being sprayed on the eyes, it is better not to teach it this trick. Your dog may react negatively if you insist on teaching it something he does not like.

Go To Your Spot

This trick is necessary to get your dog to unwind and have some time alone to itself. It will allow your dog to get away from all the attention and relax his tired muscles. You can start teaching it the command by first preparing a comfortable spot for it. It can be a dog bed or a rug.

Now say 'go to your spot' and lead your dog to their spot. Make it sit there for a while. When he is calm and still praise and treat it before releasing it. Gradually increase the staying time for your dog. Soon your dog will be accustomed to its spot and you will not need to lead it there. Simply throw a treat from far and call out 'go to your spot.' Make sure your dog sits on the spot for a while before leaving. You can encourage it by giving it a juicy bone to enjoy while he relaxes on his spot.

After your dog has learnt the trick, he will go there on command but he will also go there by itself when he feels the need to relax and rest.

Yawn

For this trick you will have to wait for your dog to actually yawn before teaching it to it. You will have to be patient and keep a watch on your dog until he yawns. When your dog actually yawns, say 'yawn' or 'are you sleepy.' Praise your dog a lot and treat it generously whenever he yawns to let it know he was doing something wonderful.

If your dog yawns a lot, it will be able to learn the trick sooner. After some practice sessions, your dog will yawn whenever you tell it to. This trick can be followed by the 'go to your spot' trick when your dog is tired and needs some rest.

c. How Teaching Tricks to Your Dog Will Help You

- You will be able to control his behavior. This will enable you to take your canine to public places like parks or to someone's home without the fear of your dog getting out of hand.

- Teaching your dog a few tricks will allow a two-way communication between you and your pet. You both will be able to understand each other better and your dog will become more obedient in the process.

- Most dogs are very energetic and need to release their physical energy in some way. Training your dog to perform tricks will not only calm your dog but will also allow it to constructively release his energy. This way your dog will learn and you both can have some fun too.

- Some people fear having dogs around them. If you have friends who are afraid of dogs, you can put them at ease with having your dog to perform some tricks for them. They will soon forget their fear and join in the fun with you and your dog.

- Dog tricks are also known as "alternate behavior". This is because they allow you to control your dog's behavior. If your dog accompanies you to a new place and gets nervous on meeting new people, he may start barking or jump on your friends. You can distract your pet by calling out a command like 'play dead' or 'roll over' to distract it from the current situation and get it busy in other things.

- The best thing about teaching your dog tricks is that you can show it off to your friends. Dogs love being admired and if his tricks get it admired and praised, he will surely not shy away from performing these tricks in front of new people.

d. Points to Be Wary Of

- Always allow your dog to clearly understand the step and respond to it properly. Teaching your dog in a rush may make it irritable and he may not respond properly. Ensure your dog is in a playful mood when you begin to teach it new tricks.

- Some dogs do not listen and become very frustrating for their owners. It is best to teach them with patience as well as treat them and praise their every move.

- It is best to teach your dog tricks when it is still a puppy. Young pups learn faster and respond well. If your dog has grown up, you can still teach it tricks, but you will have to be patient with it as it may take time to learn and respond.

- Do not overdo with the treats when your dog has learnt the tricks. Use hand signals to make your dog obey you and continuously praise and pet it when he follows your commands. This will allow your dog to become more accustomed to your verbal commands and hand signals.

- Keep the training treats with you wherever you take your dog. Continuously practicing the commands with your pet will make it learn them easily. Feed it treats from time to time to keep it motivated. If you only tell it to perform tricks without treating it, he may lose interest in the activity.

- You can also use other training tools like clickers and target sticks to train your dog better. These are easily available at your local pet store. If you cannot find them, it is absolutely fine as they are not a necessity. Your hand signals, verbal commands and training treats will be enough to train your dog.

e. How to make your dog listen to you?

If you think your dog does not listen to you and goes on doing as he pleases, then you may see if the answer to any of the below questions is in the negative or positive:

1- Do you use collars, cookies, clickers or head halters to make your Caucasian Shepherd listen to you?
2- Do you have to be loud whenever you want your dog to listen to you?
3- Does your dog always obey your commands, and at any place?

If the answers to the above are all in the negative, then you need to take your training role seriously, establish yourself as the alpha figure in the relationship and come off as an ideal pet parent.

Once you have established the alpha role, make sure your dog knows its name. If your Caucasian Shepherd does not know its name, then you cannot have its attention for teaching any other commands.

In order to ensure that your dog recognizes its name, use a treat. Take the treat in your hand and hold it at a distance from your body. Call out your dog's name. It will most probably look at the treat in your hand. Continue to call out its name until it looks square at your eyes. Once it does that, give the treat to the dog immediately. Do the same by taking the treat in your other hand. Once you are certain that your dog knows its name, just call it out and reward it for looking at you by hugging it or petting it.

10. Breeding

If you are considering breeding your dog, talk to a breeder first. Ask it about the pitfalls, problems, expenses and likely disappointments. Also get your bitch examined by an expert first. There are also some questions you need to ask yourself before you resort to breeding:

1- Have you bred large dogs before? It is not as automatic as one may assume.
2- Can you pay all the expenses?
3- Will you test prior to the pregnancy?
4- Are you prepared to care for a pregnant bitch?
5- Can you afford a cesarean if it comes to it?
6- The bitch may die. Can you handle parting from your pet?
7- Have you hand fed a litter before?
8- Can you watch the litter 24/7 to ensure that your gigantic bitch does not roll over and suffocate them?
9- Are you willing to line up and invest in a veterinarian?

10- Suppose all your puppies are not sold off by 8 weeks of age. What will you do then?

11- Can you afford the subsequent vaccinations, food and care of the unsold litter?

12- Can you house, housebreak, train and socialize all of your litter in case you cannot sell them right away?

The above questions are not meant to discourage breeding, but they should definitely be addressed before you get into breeding.

Remember, you should breed your dog only if the following conditions are met:

1- The dog meets an approved standard of breeding

2- You have ensured the above by having your dog examined by not one, but more experts.

3- You are mentally prepared to look after all of the litter in case they are not sold.

4- You are willing to retrieve the puppy or dog you have bred in case it comes to it. If you think you can make money off breeding, reclaim your purchasing price and the expenses on the dog, then you cannot be more wrong. Dog breeding is not a casual venture. You need to talk to experts first, preferably in animal shelters, and weigh in the pros and cons before getting into the whole breeding business.

11. Walking

The Caucasian Ovcharka is a large dog with a lot of energy. It requires a lot of exercise and will be happiest in a home that has a lot of free space. They need a job to do – they are protectors and guards by nature. They might even take care of their own exercise while on job. But in case you have not given them a job, they will need a good long walk to let their energy out. When walking your Caucasian, make them heel beside you or behind you. If you let it lead, it will assume the alpha role and give you a tough time listening to you.

There is a myth about those dogs living in private houses not needing any walking. Know that lack of exercise will result in sagged backs and easily fatigued dogs.

12. Socializing

The Caucasian Shepherds need to be socialized in order to tame them. The process of socialization has to start from the moment of their birth. It has to start within the house and then taken outside.

They should be socialized with a range of animals. It can be the other house pet or all of your children at home. You can then move on to familiarize them with frequently visiting friends and family members.

Proper socialization helps teach the Caucasian Shepherd the right time to guard and defend, and also helps to familiarize them with the sights and sounds of the modern world. If this isn't done, then chances are that your dog will get startled by the next approaching car or a new face in the house. They can be pretty loud with their barking, and therefore, you cannot afford to have them do so very frequently. Ongoing socialization is essential in order to prevent behavioral problems. It should occur throughout your dog's lifetime. It prevents aggression and fearful behavior. No socialization will lead to barking, shyness, hyperactive behavior and aggression. The younger you start socializing your dog, the better all dogs can be socialized and be made to enjoy fearful situations.

As these dogs mature, they begin to display their guarding instincts and the owner must strive to correct and praise every incident as he or she deems fit. This refers to supervising lunging, barking or roaring at 2:00 am or at 2:00 pm. They must be taught the distinction in barking levels as per varying extents of threats. A person minding his own business on a public sidewalk is not a threat by any means and a bark or two should alert the owner. Someone walking up your doorway is a likely threat and would require a different intensity of barking. Your dog will not know this by default, and therefore you will have to teach it that.

Following are some guidelines for you when exposing your dog to something new or something it is wary of:

- Remain calm and up-beat. If it is wearing a leash, keep it loose.
- Make sure the exposure to a certain thing it is fearful of, is gradual. Do not force it to accept the new object. If it retreats, let it.
- Reward your dog if it is calm and has explored the new situation positively.

You should attempt to expose your dog to the things and situations it is likely to come across in the future. The key is to proceed slowly so that your dog enjoys these sessions. You might think it is taking a lot of your time but do know that it's a good investment of your time. You will get a very well-behaved dog at the end. There are some examples given below:

- Have it meet all kinds of people, e.g. children, women, men, crowds, disabled people, people wearing hats, those with beards, etc.
- Have it meet other dogs but if you have a puppy, do not bring it near other dogs until after 4 months due to risk of contracting a disease. If it is a well-run puppy kindergarten, then it's a different story.
- Expose the dog to other pets if you own any, e.g. cats, birds, horses, etc.
- Enable and teach it to enjoy and play with its crate
- Take it for rides in the car but ensure restraining it with a secured crate or a dog seatbelt.
- Make your dog used to being held, petted and touched all over. This includes being bathed and groomed.
- Have it accustomed to visiting the veterinarian's office, the day care, the groomer or the boarding kennel.

- It should be used to hearing loud noises and strange objects like opening an umbrella or passage of a low flying airplane.
- While taking it on walks, expose it to traffic, motorcycles, skateboards, joggers and bicycles. These things will otherwise be threatening aliens for your dog, which it might attack. Even if it sees these things from a distance, it will start barking uncontrollably.
- Leave it alone for a few hours at a time so it does not get separation anxiety too easily.

The following Do's and Don'ts can be a good way to moderate your own behavior while socializing your dog:

Do's

- Invite people owning friendly puppies and dogs to your own home so they can play with your puppy.

- Introduce new things to the puppy every day.

- Puppies get tired easily. Give your puppy space of its own where it will sleep and relax.

- Have your puppy use the stairs after introducing them to the puppy.

- Reward your dog with treats for even the smallest improvement in behaviour.

- Be patient.

Don'ts

- Do not be lazy. You will have to keep trying new things daily in order to establish a lasting relationship with your dog.

- Don't push the dog into learning fast. Introduce it to new things, but give it time to get familiar and accustomed to them.

- Do not bombard it with information by introducing too many things at the same time. It is essential to keep it slow. You may be excited about training your puppy, but you might end up confusing it if you try too many things with it at once.

- Do not introduce the puppy with unfamiliar dogs at the onset. Adult dogs can be very territorial and they might scare your puppy into not leaving the house at all.

13. Poison Control

It would be a good idea to plan ahead before you buy your dog and bring it to the house. An experienced dog owner will probably say that you can never be prepared enough, but it is possible to be planned ahead for any serious or common emergencies. There are many toxic hazards for dogs and it is important that you keep them away from your dog.

Poisonous substances for dogs include certain foods and plants. All the toxins are far too many to mention here, but we will state here whichever ones are most important and commonly found in homes. If you are not sure about a substance, check with the vet or an animal organization like the ASPCA.

a. Inside Plants

The following plants are generally placed inside the house or in the yard where the dog might have access to them. If you have any of them, please either relinquish them or relocate them to another place in your house where the dog cannot go, e.g. in the shed or a greenhouse, if you have one. Yet, the best thing to do would be to remove them altogether.

- Caladium
- Dumbcane
- Aloe Vera
- Yew
- Chrysanthemum
- Emerald Fern
- Elephant's Ear
- Hyacinth
- Philodendron
- Weeping Fig

b. Outside Plants:

The following plants which will be placed outside, should be kept away from the dog's access:

- Ivy
- Azaleas
- Foxglove
- Daffodils
- Morning Glory
- Nightshade

- Green Potato
- Oak
- Wisteria
- Rhododendrum

c. Human Foods:

The following foods are commonly consumed by humans, and therefore, may be found lying around the house, especially if you have children. It is important to eat them responsibly and dispose of them properly.

- Fruit Seeds and Pits: Most of them contain cyanide which can kill your dog.
- Avocado: All of its parts are poisonous for dogs. Make sure you dispose off the pit properly in case your dog hovers near trash.
- Garlic: This contains a small amount of thiosulphate, which can be toxic. A lot of it may have to be taken to poison a dog, but the problem is that it builds up in the system and can cause problems in the long run.
- Chocolate: It contains a cardiac stimulant known as theobromine, which can be fatal to dogs.
- Macadamia Nuts: They affect the dog's nervous system and can prove to be fatal.
- Grapes: They are lethal for dog's kidneys and can therefore, cause excruciating pain before killing it.
- Onions: They contain the same toxic substance as garlic, but in much larger amounts.
- Sugar-Free foods: Xylitol, which is a component of these foods, can cause liver failure in your dog.
- Raisins: Same problem with them as grapes.

- Tomatoes: They contain oxalates which can be poisonous for dogs.
- Potatoes
- Rhubarb
- Mushrooms: They affect the heart, kidneys and the nervous system.

d. Miscellaneous

The following products are always lying around the house and some may even be deliberately given to dogs, but they can cause more damage than good:

- Prescription medicines for humans: They can have an opposite effect on dogs. Most common ones are anti-inflammatory and pain medications; anti-depressants and blood pressure medications.
- Tick and flea products: If ingested, they can kill dogs. Even application of excessive amounts can kill small puppies.
- Insecticides
- Over-the-counter medications: Products with acetaminophen, ibuprofen and naproxen (e.g. Tylenol and Advil) can be poisonous for dogs. Similarly, nutraceutical products and herbal supplements can also be bad for dogs.
- Many pet medications can also kill dogs due to adverse reaction, just like it happens to humans. Examples of such medications can be pain killers and dewormers.
- House hold products like antifreeze, paint thinners, pool chemicals can make dogs really sick through stomach and respiratory tract problems.
- Rodenticides
- Lawn and garden products

80

e. Hazards for Dogs during the Holidays

Holidays are busy and hectic times for dog owners and their entire families. They may miss out some of the poisonous stuff lying around which may prove to be detrimental to the dog's health or cause its demise. These things include the following:

- Christmas Plants: Many plants used for decoration during Christmas can be toxic to dogs. They include Poinsettias, Holly and Mistletoe. Look for safer substitutes so your dog doesn't suffer.
- July fourth: Alcohol can be toxic for dogs, so make sure the dog isn't given any or doesn't have access to it during those BBQs.
- Thanksgiving: Too much fat can be toxic for dogs, especially if consumed in a short period of time. Therefore, turkey should be trimmed well and the gravy to be kept exclusively for the humans only.
- Easter: Tulips and lilies both are poisonous for dogs.
- Halloween: Excessive sugar intake, as well as chocolate, can be fatal for dogs.

f. Signs of toxicity

Each kind of toxin has its own sign, but the most common signs are given below:

- Diarrhea
- Coma
- Abdominal pain – the way to gauge this is that the dog will whine and its stomach will be soft to touch.
- Convulsions
- Lethargy
- Drooling

- Irregular heartbeat
- Vomiting
- Swollen Limbs
- Labored breathing

g. What to do in case of suspected dog poisoning?

If you feel your dog is poisoned, the first thing to do is to remain calm. Act quickly but rationally. Follow the following steps:

- Gather the remaining poison to show it to vet. It'll help him make an informed decision faster. If the dog has vomited, collect the vomit too to show it to the doctor.
- Calm your dog and call the vet or the ASPCA (Animal Poison Control Centre (APCC) in you are in the US, or an similar body that functions in your country.
- There are home remedies like charcoal and sodium sulphate, but its best to get a vet's advice before helping your dog.

f. Poison-protection: Pet-proofing your Home

You can make your house safe for your pet, by doing the following:

- Keep all medications in cabinets, even the child-proof bottles.
- Search and pick up any and all pills you accidently drop on the floor
- Supervise children and elderly when they take their medication
- Always follow guidelines on labels for flea or tick products
- Ask your vet about any foods you are not sure about

- For your dog, only give it treats made specifically for dogs
- All rodenticides should be kept in cabinets or high in shelves so your pet cannot find them
- Keep only those plants in your house that are not fatal for your dog. The ASPCA website has a list of such plants. Many of the common ones are stated above too.
- All cleaners and chemicals should be kept in those areas of your home, where your pet cannot access them
- Always keep the contact number of pet poison control authority or the vet handy in case of emergencies.

14. Spaying and Neutering

Spaying is the term used for the ovariohysterectomy of a female animal. Neutering is the castration of a male animal but this term may also be used for females sometimes. Both of them are surgical procedures and have to be performed by a vet. They will render an animal from ever reproducing. Following are some aspects that you need to know about spaying or neutering:

a. When to get it done?
Both these procedures can be performed when the animal is as young as 8 weeks old. It is actually preferred to have this procedure done early since it is healthy and also reduces the risk of pet overpopulation.

b. Why do it?
Both private and public animal shelters are facing the tremendous burden of pet overpopulation. There just aren't enough good homes for all of them. If you do not get your pet neutered, you will be adding to this burden, if not for the authorities, then yourself.

c. What are the behavioral and health benefits related to these procedures?

Spaying will alleviate the constant crying and nervousness of a dog in heat, and will also eliminate the mess that comes with the heat cycle.

Neutering will prevent many distasteful sexual behaviors like humping, urine marking, the urge to roam or male aggression. If you have many dogs, it is best you get them neutered, or there will be a lot of fighting for mates.

A long-term benefit is the improved health for dogs. Neutering the males prevents testicular cancer, enlargement of the prostate gland and also reduces the risk of getting perianal tumors.

d. But it costs too much!

This will be a one-time expense and will go a long way. If you do not get this done, then be prepared to bear the feeding, vet, deworming and grooming costs for the litter of pups you will have if your pet was not spayed. You can find low-cost spaying and neutering options in local animal shelters. You can also always go to the vet to get it done.

e. Not even one litter for my purebred?

Purebred or not, there just aren't enough homes for those puppies. Unless you have designated homes decided beforehand, and are willing to take adequate care of unsold ones, get them neutered right away. Know that 25% of the shelter dogs are purebreds. You will face a lot of trouble getting them a home if you breed them irresponsibly.

f. If I find them a home, then its okay, right?

No. For every puppy that you give away to a willing adopter, you are robbing the home of an animal already in a home. Many animals have to be euthanized because they cannot be given proper homes. Nobody wants to add to that.

g. So my female dog cannot even have one litter?

No. She will be much healthier if she does not mature sexually.

h. Does neutering change the personality of the pet?

Not really. Even if there are behavioral changes, they are probably for the best. It will not be roaming around looking for a mate and will be much less aggressive.

Chapter 6. Annual Cost of Keeping a Caucasian Shepherd

This dog sure has special requirements when it comes to socialization and training but its cost of keeping is almost the same as other dogs if you discount the cost of a training school in case you decide to use one. The average cost of ownership can range from $1200-$1500 or £700-£900 to a year and the main cost would be food unless your dog has medical problems in which case the medical costs can take the figure up by much higher. The lifetime commitment when it comes to finances can range from $10,000 to $15,000 or £6000 to . If you cannot afford to allocate this much money on a pet just yet, then wait till you can. Cutting back on the dog expenses can mean depriving it of proper care and diet, and that can result in the dog getting sick or even dying.

The below table will highlight some of the costs associated with owning the dog:

Sr. No	Particular	Estimated Cost ($/month)
1	Food, supplement (Nupro) and Treats	35
2	Accessories (collars, tags and leashes)	10-20
3	Veterinary Care:	
	Wellness exam, office visit & annual vaccinations	80-100 (average)
	Spay/ neuter	300-500 (differs with geographical location and maturity of female)
	Worming*	20-50
	External parasite treatment**	20-40
	Heartworm***	Heartgard or interceptor
	If dog is HW positive	300-600
	Other illness (serious and hospitalization needed)	400-1000+
4	Boarding	20-30 (off peak) 30-40 (on peak days)
5	Basic obedience classes or other behavior modification classes	50-100 (optional for fosters)

* Eliminates hookworms, tapeworms, roundworms, coccidia and whip worms, etc.

**Flea and ticks; skin condition (mostly mites) and grooming

***This is preventative as long as the dog is tested negative to this test

Chapter 7. Some General How-Tos

Below are some guidelines for you to refer to when faced with a situation. These situations can be related to house training, behavior control or medical issues.

1. Potty-Train Your Dog

Potty training your dog would be the first step in making it fit for polite company. Many people see it as a hassle while some take it as a challenge. But the truth is that it is a part and parcel of owning a dog. There is no gain without a little bit of pain, and if you do a good job with your Caucasian in potty training, you will not have any accidents in the house. It is very gratifying to see your training coming into play when your dog does it right. But if you do not take this aspect seriously, you will have mounds of problems ranging from a frequently soiled house to health threats for yourself and your family.

a. Things to know before potty training
Note the below before proceeding to potty train your dog:

1- Understand your dog's body language. It will display special behavior when it wants to eliminate. Look out for those signs.
2- If you have puppies, remember that they will go more frequently than adult dogs. This can be as soon as they wake up either after a long sleep or short naps; after play time; after meals and being crated and definitely before sleeping at night.

3- Take your dog for a walk when it needs to go potty. A yard would be a good place where it can relieve itself. Take it there every night and it will know its defecating area.

4- Praise your Caucasian Shepherd when he eliminates in the right place. Treats are even better. But the key is to reward it every time it does it right. This is positive reinforcement and will make the dog abide by your rules for defecation venues.

5- Try signal training after a while. This will tell you when your dog wants to go potty. This can be done by hanging a bell at its level near the dog and teaching it to push it with its nose or patting it with its paw.

6- Until and unless your dog is completely potty trained, keep a strict eye on it. Do not let it roam around in the house freely.

7- Try using a crate. A dog trained with a crate is happy to get its own den. The benefit that comes from crating is that dogs do not soil the place where they sleep and so it will not eliminate in the crate.

8- Try litter pan training if you live in a high rise and do not have a back yard. The idea is to create a place within the house where the dog can relieve itself.

9- Do not scold or hit your dog when training it. Only use positive reinforcement. If you catch it doing something wrong, a stern 'FREEZE' or 'NO' would do.

10- Do not keep your dog along for more than 4 hours. If you do, be prepared to return to a soiled home since separation anxiety is very common among home alone dogs.

11- Sudden accidents may happen due to medical problems or health disorders. Do not discount them. But it is unlikely for a Caucasian Shepherd to act out of habit otherwise.

12- Many dogs are known to mark their territory by urinating in the respective area. It can be a wall or the leg of a table.

Simply clean the area and use a deodorant to stave off the smell.

13- Be patient and know that house training a Caucasian Shepherd takes time. If you persevere, you will end up having a great housetrained Caucasian Mountain Dog.

b. Potty Training a Puppy

No matter what the breed is, housetraining a puppy is a very tough task. It does not develop full control over its bladder until it is 4 or 5 months old. Because they are growing and developing rapidly, they eat more, burn more and even eliminate more frequently than an adult Caucasian Shepherd.

After each meal, nap, play or drink, take your puppy to the designated area for defecation, and stay there till it relieves itself. Then bring it to its crate. Repeat this act every day until it develops a habit of doing so.

c. Potty Training an Adult Caucasian Mountain Dog

The best way to train a fully grown or adult Caucasian Shepherd is to begin from scratch. Observe it closely and maintain a record of when it goes and where. Note when it poops- when you are out or in. Time yourself to be at home when it feels the need to go. You can try crate training but be careful to introduce it gradually to the dog.

2. Take Care of Pregnant Female Dogs

Metabolic disorders, disorders of internal organs and improper care can lead to complications in pregnancy and child birth. But be wary of false pregnancy, which can occur if the sexual cycle is not accompanied by mating. Symptoms of false pregnancy are the same as normal pregnancy: sense of excitement in the dog; increase in the abdomen and appearance of milk. You should take your dog to the vet and he or she will prescribe some sedative drugs. Milk and dairy products should be eliminated from the dog's diet.

Toxicosis may occur in the dog during real pregnancy. The symptoms may include weakness, depression, vomiting and loss of appetite. It is important to change the diet of the pregnant dog as per the vet's orders. If you feed your dog improperly and if the dog lacks physical activity, then edema may occur. There may be some swelling in the hind legs and around the mammary glands. If this occurs, reduce the amount of fluid in the diet; refrain from over feeding your dog; walk it regularly and massage the area where edema is seen.

Sometimes the dog may experience weakening in labor. This may be caused by multiple gestations or large scale gestations, and even poor health of the animal. Due to weak contractions, or weak uterine and abdominal muscles, puppies' birth may be delayed. A vet must be called right away but meanwhile, give the pup a warm drink and a massage.

You must call the vet if you see any of the following symptoms:

1- No signs of labor after the due date has passed
2- The fetus is stuck in the birth canal
3- Still born pups
4- Discontinued labor despite presence of more fetus in the womb
5- Placenta retained after the puppies' birth
6- The dog fights but does not push the fetus out.

a. What to Feed your Pregnant Dog?

What should you feed your dog during the pregnancy and growth stages? Formula food is a good idea. So whatever type of food you are feeding them, there is usually a puppy type variant as well, and it is just in smaller bits for puppies that helps avoid choking.

At the same time, when a puppy is growing they need more protein in their diet. And even the pregnant female needs protein, nutrients, and calcium. Puppy food works well in this regard.

One of the best medications when they are pregnant is Fenbendazole. It is also called Safe-Guard. This is a worm prevention medicine. It is safe and can be given to your dog constantly while she is pregnant.

b. Whelping

First things First

A whelping box is really nice. You can purchase it, or build one yourself. This allows the mother to get out of the box, but keeps the puppies contained in one place. If you are going to build a whelping box, make sure it is about three times the size of the mother dog.

This will give you room for the puppies, but mom can also move away easily after feeding them. She also gets the necessary space to stretch out. Also, this allows you to put a heating pad under one side so that the bottom will be warm for the puppies. When they are warm enough, they can move to the cooler side. Warmth allows them to digest food. You will also need clean towels right after the birthing process.

Caution

When the mother goes into labor, you should not give her too much attention, or attempt to grab the puppies. Too much attention may cause the mom to stress, and she may attempt to hide her puppies. Doing so, she can either smother them or kill them. So you do not want to give her too much attention, but be there to assist if she needs you.

The Birth Time Frame

She will have her babies in 60-65 days (63 on average) after tying with a male. This will be normal time she will have her puppies. However, be ready one week in advance. Have her in the whelping box where she can have her puppies.

If nothing happens after 65 days that is a red flag. If there are no signs of puppies, but she still feels in her mid-section, you need to get her to a vet and have her checked out. It could be a sign of complications. There are ways to tell, such as X-rays, although these can be expensive.

Birth – Signs of What's to Come

You will notice she starts nesting. This means she will begin to find a place she can have puppies. If you already have a whelping box setup and she is sleeping there, this will be the perfect place for her. You will notice as she is nesting she will lie around more, and be uncomfortable. She will move around a lot and won't be able to relax. If you see she is uncomfortable, the puppies will be coming soon.

Temperature change

A dog's normal body temperature is around 101.5 degrees. However, her body temperature will drop to 99 degrees a few hours before the puppies are coming. This is a clear sign.

The way you can test for this is to take the thermometer, and use a lot of Vaseline or any other lubricant. Just make sure that the thermometer is sanitary. Place it in her rectum, and leave it for about 30 seconds up to a minute.

Instant temperature readings work as well. You will be able to notice her temperature drop and know the puppies are coming.

Contractions and Panting

As soon as labor starts, she will begin to pant, hang her tongue out, and become tired. This cools her body, but is a sign of her contractions as well. You can give them yogurt or cottage cheese. The calcium will help her produce milk.

Also, it helps her contractions, making them stronger and also helps during the healing process afterwards. She may not want to eat it, so don't force it. Don't give large amounts.

Watch closely

When she is in labor, let her do the work. There is no need to freak out and think you need to be there and be hands on. Let the mom relax and do her job. Your job is to be there to watch and assist if anything goes wrong. But do not take over or try to do things for her.

Steps of Birth

When the mom starts to go into labor, you will notice a discharge from her vulva. This is a sign her body is preparing for birth, and the discharge acts as a lubricant to help the puppies get out. Then also all of those fluids are working their way out.

Puppies will come out in a sac. The mom will then need to clean and stimulate the puppy. So she will remove the sac and she usually does that with her teeth. She will then clean the puppy, stimulating it, getting the mucus off of its face, and licking it, moving its tummy and rubbing it.

This stimulates the puppy into breathing. The mom will then cut the umbilical by chewing it off the puppy at its tummy. Sometimes when she does this, she will pick the puppy up off of the ground by the umbilical cord, and it is okay.

On the other side of the umbilical cord is the afterbirth and placenta. The mom will eat the placenta, and this is OK for her. But she doesn't need to eat all of them. If you notice she is eating all of them or having trouble swallowing them, don't be afraid to take the placenta away and throw it away.

Afterbirth and placenta can be nourishing for the mother, giving her nourishment for feeding the puppies. Too many can make her sick, and she may throw them up and then eat them again. If you feel the need, you can take the afterbirth away from her. It will take her mind off of them. She doesn't need to eat all of them, but it is OK if she does.

Sometimes when the mom chews off the umbilical cord, the other end of that cord is left inside her. It is okay for you to grab that umbilical cord and gently pull as it is not attached to her, and then the afterbirth will come out. To be sure, simply count the number of puppies and match them with the number dog afterbirths.

Finally, once a puppy is born, it will attempt to nurse. It is OK for you place that puppy on the mother and help them nurse. This will help to stimulate her nipples and help her relieve contractions.

Your Role During the Birth Process

If the mom doesn't break the sac, then it is your responsibility to break it. If the puppy comes out and the sac is on the puppy too long, the puppy could suffocate. You're going to pinch the sac and open it.

Secondly, if the mom is having too many puppies at once and can't focus on all of them, feel free to help her. If the sac is already broken, she may not notice the puppy still needs to be stimulated. If the puppy comes out and the sac breaks on the way out, she may just miss it, so you will want to stimulate the puppy putting it under her nose so she sees it.

This will help in the survival of puppies. If she doesn't chew off the umbilical cord- either because she misses it or is overwhelmed by puppies-you can assist by helping her cut the cord.

There are different ways. Some people will tie it off, others will cut it. I personally will pinch an inch, and then tear it because that doesn't leave a clean cut that will bleed. If she steps in at that point, then let her take over. So just watch and help if needed, pay attention that the umbilical cord doesn't continue to bleed. You do not want the puppy to bleed to death. This is a possibility. So if it doesn't stop bleeding tie a piece of string on it.

Warning Signs

If the dog is in labor for 6 hours with no puppies, call the veterinarian. They may advise you over the phone and don't charge you all. A puppy can be stuck in the birth canal and prevent the others from being able to come out. Dogs usually have smooth births, so call the vet if you notice any complications.

Don't Stress

This is the most important lesson. Normally the dog will take care of the whole process. You can even view dog birthing videos on the Internet.

3. Take Care of Newborn Puppies

Taking care of adorable puppies born in your home can be rewarding, fun and stressful at the same time. You will hear them cry and whine as they will begin to settle down in their new environment. Take care of them, ensure their comfort and provide them with their basic needs not only because they are the little ones of your beloved dogs, but also because you want to keep them healthy and increase their survival in the best possible manner during their first weeks of life so that you are able to sell them for top dollar.

The following information will help you provide the best living conditions to newborn pups at home.

Tips for Newborns

Things you need to arrange soon after the pups are born:

First of all, setup a warm and large nesting area for the little pups as well as for the mothers inside your house. You can get a children's wading pool or a large box to create one. Make sure it isn't too high and allows easy access and exit for the mother. If you can arrange, keep the box in a warm room with temperature as high as 80°F during the initial days. Do not setup the nesting area outdoors and keep the pups inside for at least the first few weeks.

Before placing the puppies in the box (nesting area), line it with clean, soft towels that are not in your use. The towels are essential as they provide the necessary insulation and warmth. Now cover this soft surface with layers of newspaper, which will allow you to remove the waste easily. Once this is done, place the pups inside carefully.

Use a gentle cleanser to clean the lining of the box at least twice in a week. Be very careful when choosing the cleanser, as fumes can be harmful and irritating to little puppies. Look for a cleanser that has the least amount of perfume and dye possible.

Make sure the puppies are nursing properly. For the first week, they should nurse after every two hours. In case the mother is not present and puppies are not nursing adequately, learn to feed them a bottle with replacer milk.

Tip: You will find your newborn puppies sleeping most of the time. Do not allow the mother to be absent for longer than necessary. During the initial weeks, keep her water and food supplies closer to her newborn babies so she stays near them as much as possible.

Adjusting With the Pups

Aside from arranging the place to rest, the take of little puppies is the responsibility of their mother and she will take care of their feeding and cleanliness needs herself. However, as they will grow, you will need to ensure you are providing them the most comfortable environment, where they are in their best health conditions.

The following points will help you learn how to adjust with the pups as they start to grow.

Puppy-Proof Your Environment

Little puppies are explorers. They usually do that by using their mouth. Therefore, it is very important that you keep your pup as well as your house safe. In order to do so, you will need to take a few precautions. If your puppies are indoors and free to roam around, remove all breakable things they can access. Keep windows closed (especially low ones) and electrical cords covered or raised. Keep cleaning and toxic chemicals/supplies away from the reach of puppies. Also, replace your old trash can with a taller, heavier trash can that is too tall and heavy for your puppy to knock over. Keep your puppy confined in a certain room or area by installing a folding gate.

Get Necessary Supplies

Place their bed in the bathroom or kitchen because that place is usually warm and can be washed easily. The following list of things will help you get started:

1. Metal Bowls: Grab two metal bowls for water and food for your little puppies. They are better than glass because they stay cleaner and do not chip.

2. Bed for Pups: You need to have a place for your puppies to sleep. Your options include a snuggle nest, a crate pillow, or a wicker basket lined with soft towels. Keep their bedding dry, comfy and soft. When the weather is cold, keep a blanket.

3. Lots of toys: Little puppies are like energy thunderbolt. Get plenty of toys for them to play with. Get some soft toys and chew toys as well. However, make sure they are designed for puppies and are indestructible or else your puppy can even choke and die.

4. Treats: Treat here does not include chocolates. Do not include anything that you know is poisonous for your dogs. However, keep a variety and provide soft and crunchy treats. Crunchy will help the little pups clean their teeth while soft is great for training.

5. Food Supply: Depending on the breed you have, you will need to do some research about the food. Kibble, home cooked, canned and raw diets are all options available for you. Whichever food you decide to give those little adorable creatures, make sure it is free of preservatives, artificial flavors and dyes. Your puppies might be allergic to these.

6. Grooming Tools: You need to grab a few things you just cannot ignore. These include towels, toothbrush, dog

toothpaste, dog conditioner, dog shampoo, nail clippers, rubber gloves, comb and bristle brush.

7. A Tag and Harness: Get a metal tag and a nylon harness for your pups. It can injure their throat and can hurt their necks. When adjusting the size of the harness, remember the puppies will grow.

Make the Puppies Comfortable

Although they were born in the same home, you need to make them comfortable with the environment they are in as they grow up. Shower your love and attention to your puppy and he will love you back. You can keep their beds or box in your room to keep a watch over them and they will not feel alone or isolated.

Allow your puppies to access different areas of your home at times. This will help them get familiar with the routes and ways within the house. Let your puppy play around, it will help them grow healthy.

Love Them

They belong to you until they are sold and so they are your pets. Treat them in a nice way and stroke their bodies, heads, and legs several times in a day. Not only will this make your pups feel loved, but they will also behave and follow your commands.

Puppies are fragile, just like little human babies. You are responsible to take care of them and protect them. Also, you need to be careful while handling them. Do not allow little children to pick them up or hurt their little, fragile bodies. Gently scoop your little pup if you want to pick it up. Always support by keeping one hand under it while you are holding it.

Protect Them

Regardless of what breed you have, when they are small, all puppies are curious by nature. They love to explore and do not hesitate in trespassing the line if they are not watched. There is a chance they might get lost sometimes. Therefore, it is important to make your puppies wear collars. Get a soft, comfortable collar for all your puppies and adjust it according to their neck size. Also, make sure you gradually loosen it to adjust for their growth. Also, place a tag in the collar with your name, phone number or address. This will come in handy in case your puppy gets lost.

Allow your puppies to play in a safe, secluded area. If you wish to keep them outdoors, a securely-fenced yard will be perfect. Place their toys in that area and there will be fewer chances they will want to move away.

Feeding the Little Pups

Here comes the most important part of raising pups – feeding. You need to provide the best of feeding to keep them in good health.

The Right Puppy Food

During the first few weeks, the mother dog will take care of the feeding needs of her pups. However, once they start growing, you need to provide them with proper puppy food that is equally nourishing for them.

While many people find it tempting to grab the cheap stuff when it comes to feeding an animal, it is important to understand that by doing so you are keeping the life of your puppy at risk. Indeed cheap food is not the right choice for the little dog you have.

Search for food items that incorporate proteins in high quality from fish, eggs, lamb and/or chicken.

Your puppies also need to consume fatty acids to maintain its healthy and shiny coat. Generally, the ideal ratio for your dog feed will be 5:1 omega 5 to omega 3 fatty acids. This is usually available in supplements or in food like salmon oil, especially for your puppies/dogs.

Just like human beings, you need to give them a balanced diet and fulfill their nutrition requirements in order to keep them in great health.

Feeding Them Properly

Now that you have the right puppy food with you, feed them in small amounts multiple times in a day. As mentioned earlier, dry food is good for them, as it helps them lessen gum disease and keep their teeth clean. As far as the amount of food is concerned, it completely depends on the age of your puppies and their breed. Research and look for recommendations from experts for your specific breed.

If there is a range recommended, feed the smallest amount on the scale to your puppies according to its size, age and breed and gradually increase the portion if your dog seems too hungry or too thin. Again, their age will determine the number of times you need to feed them.

Six-eight weeks – four times in a day

Twelve to twenty weeks – three times in a day

Twenty+ weeks – twice a day

Avoid Buffet Feeding

If you want to follow a healthy way to feed your puppies, do not give them food in a buffet style. Of course, it is easier to simply fill up a bowl and give it to your puppies and allow them to eat as many times as they like during the day, it can affect their health. Puppies will keep eating until the food finishes. They do not really know when to stop. Thus, do not provide a lot of food at once.

In addition to food, provide adequate amounts of water to your puppies. Make sure the water is clean and fresh. Unlike food, water should always be available to them. Keep a bowl full of water that they can access at all times. Also, beware that your puppies may want to pee soon after they consume a lot of water. To avoid mess and accidents at home, take them out immediately.

Keep Harmful Food Away

Your little puppies will be all around you, playing and barking, when you are at the table enjoying your own food. While it is really tempting to feed everything you eat to your dog, doing so can affect their health and make them unhealthy and obese. In fact, chocolate, salt, avocados, onions, garlic, alcohol, tea, raisins, and grapes, among the rest, are poisonous for your puppies and dogs. These things and food prepared with any of these ingredients should not be given to puppies.

In addition to being toxic to your dog, feeding harmful food items and table scraps to your puppies can train them to trouble you more next time when you are on the table. Your puppies will start to beg and this is one habit hardest to break. Ensure good health for your pups and feed your dog food that is particularly designed for them.

Watch your puppies when they eat. This is an effective way to gauge their health. Observe if they are happy with the food. If they do not seem interested, something is surely wrong.

It is great to do some research and take recommendations from experts and vets if you have any confusion about what to feed your pups.

Health Concerns

Don't forget, you are raising these puppies so you can sell them to loving families and earn extra bucks for your income. Thus, you should also make sure they are in their best health until they are with you.

Maintain a Safe Environment

A dirty or unsafe environment can lead to detrimental effects to the overall well being of your puppies and instead of earning you money, can cost you double in veterinary bills.

Pay attention to the bedding first. Air it out on a daily basis and replace or wash it weekly. Dedicate some time to house-training your puppies and replace it immediately if they have had an accident in it.

Remove plants that could be harmful. Puppies can chew your indoor plants and most of them could be toxic to them. Keep shamrock, rhubarb, rhododendron, foxglove, yew, azalea, oleander and lily of the valley away from your puppies.

Help Them Exercise

It is important to remember that your puppies need exercise. You cannot simply lock them at home with limited space and expect them to remain healthy and active. In short, you should make sure your puppies are getting the adequate level of exercise. This will, however, vary from breed to breed. Research and find out how much exercise is essential for your particular breed and plan accordingly.

Exercise with dogs is different. They are stronger and tougher. When dealing with little pups, keep their exercise limited. Since their body is still in the development phase, do not allow them to indulge in any sort of strenuous exercise that is longer than 2 miles or rough play.

Take them to your garden or backyard once they have eaten, and allow them to play or take them for a short walk.

Allow them to enjoy at least an hour of walk in a day. For convenience, break it into 3 to 4 walks after the pups have had their meals. Allow them to play together in your yard. Let them exercise and gain confidence at the same time.

Allow your puppies to socialize, however make sure they are vaccinated. Allow them to mingle with other puppies and be friendly with other animals and grown dogs. Make sure you keep a watch throughout.

Vet Visits

Just like you look for the right physician, you need to choose the vet very carefully. Search online or check with your friends with pets for any vet recommendations. Once you have some options on the list, visit each personally and observe. Choose the one that smells clean, is well managed, and clean. Before you are satisfied, ask as many questions as you like to the staff or the vet directly (if possible). Make sure they are able to resolve your queries and satisfy you in the best of their ability. Before you decide on the right vet, be sure you are satisfied and comfortable with your choice.

Between the age of 6 and 9 weeks, you will need to take your puppies to the vet for first vaccination. Speak to the vet about parvovirus, hepatitis, canine, parainfluenza and distemper. There are more vaccines available, wait until the vet suggests you any. This will depend on the breed of your puppies as well as their specific health conditions.

De-worming medication is a must and should be given to your puppies on the first visit to the vet. In addition to be beneficial for your puppies' health, it is also important for your own. Parasites present on puppies can infect you and cause you health problems. Thus, it is important to take preventative measures.

Your next visit to the vet will be scheduled when your puppies are 12 to 16 weeks of age. This visit will be particularly to get the rabies vaccination for your puppies.

Next thing you need to ponder over is whether you want to neuter or spay your puppies. This is usually done when the puppy is around 20 weeks old. You may not need to think about it because most probably by this time your puppies will be gone to their respective homes. It will then be their decision. Of course, if you talk about your dogs, never neuter or spay them if you want to have more puppies that can later be turned into money every year.

Keep the entire record of the vet visits of all the puppies you have. This will help you sell them off at a better price.

Grooming

Taking care of the cleanliness and the coat of your puppies is your responsibility. The way your dog looks will greatly influence the buying decision of your potential customers.

Brush their Fur

Brush your puppies regularly, especially if they have a lot of fur or thick coat. It keeps them healthy and clean and allows you to keep a check on their fur and skin for any problems. The grooming and brushing products may vary by breed. Ask your veterinarian or friends with pets to suggest you the right one. Brush them all over, including their hind legs and bellies. Start brushing at a very young age to make them used to it.

Trim their Nails

You can cut the nails of your puppies at home. Start clipping their nails at an early age. Check videos on YouTube to learn the techniques or you can even ask your vet to show you. Be careful and do not hurt your puppy. Do not allow your puppies to grow long nails as it can cause strain to their own wrists as well as damage furniture, floors and even hurt people. As it is recommended, cut their nails on a weekly basis.

Teeth and Gums Health

As mentioned earlier, provide soft toys to your puppies as it helps them keep their teeth healthy. Toothpastes and toothbrushes available for puppies can also help you in keeping their teeth healthy and clean. Allow your puppies to acclimate to having their teeth brushed. Make it a pleasant and positive experience.

Bathing Schedule

It is recommended that you bath your puppies only once in a month. Washing them frequently can dry out their coat completely. If they smell bad, use scent sprays for dogs, instead.

Puppy Training

Time to train those naughty little ones before they set to a new house! People usually prefer buying a puppy that is trained and does not mess around. This is how you start:

Housebreak Your Pups

Begin housebreaking your puppies as soon as they turn 4-5 weeks. If you delay, you will have to deal with more mess. With time, it will become more challenging to train your puppies. For the first few days, you can try out using training pads. Ideally, train them to go outside the house.

Crate Training

Consider crate training as your second option. It is a helpful option for several reasons. It not only curbs bad puppy behavior, it allows you to sleep without worrying, leaving your dog alone in the house. Also, it is an effective potty training method. Make sure you use it correctly.

Basic Commands

As we all know, dogs are very good are responding to commands by nature. Who would not like to own a puppy that follows basic commands? Of course, this is an extra skill that you are teaching your puppy and of course you can sell it for top dollar. To avoid a lot of hassle, begin the command training while the puppies are young.

Some basic commands include:

- Setting a specific sound or word you want to use when you want to call your puppy.
- Teaching them to sit down when you say 'sit'.
- Teaching the puppies to lie down when you tell them to.
- If you are living with family and children, make sure everyone knows the rules they need to follow with the puppies.

4. Take Care of an Aging Dog

All breeds and even individual dogs within breeds age differently and at different times. Large breeds of dogs like Caucasians are considered a senior at 6 or 7 years of age. The best thing to do in caring for your aging dog would be to take it to a vet and asking them to sketch out a health care maintenance program for your dog. This will make aging easier for the dog.

Watch out for the following things as your dog ages:

1- Your dog will slow down as it ages. It may not always apply to all dogs, but subtle changes like delay in getting up, laying down and while using the stairs may be encountered. There might even be some stiffness and hesitation. Even some change in the weather may worsen the dog's condition. Arthritis is also common in aging dogs. It can occur in any joint - the legs, neck or back (spine). Hypothyroidism may also be the reason behind your dog slowing down. In either case, veterinary care is highly necessary. Refrain from giving any medicine without a vet's approval.

2- Graying around the muzzle and face may be encountered at 5 or 6 years of age. Premature graying may also occur at 2 years, but mostly it occurs at 5.

3- If your dog does not respond to your commands as promptly as it used to or if it gets startled if you approach it from behind, then it might be suffering from deafness. If this occurs, protect it from hazards that it may not be able to hear, like cars or kids. Dogs will learn hand signals too, and so it would be a good idea to cross train the dog well before it starts to age.

4- As dogs age, their eyes may become bluish transparent in the pupil area. This is called lenticular sclerosis. Vision may not be affected. But if there are cataracts, which are white and opaque, then consult a vet immediately.

5- There might be a mild loss in muscle mass, especially in the hind legs, as old age approaches. Muscle atrophy on the head and belly muscles can mean diseases like Cushing's Disease and Masticatory Myositis.

6- Keep your dog's teeth and gums in tip top shape. Otherwise, gingivitis may occur and this can lead to bacteria entering the bloodstream and causing other diseases.

For an aging dog, it is important to take your dog for a vet exam quite frequently. The dog should maintain a healthy weight, should be getting enough exercise both mentally or physically and should be getting a proper diet. All these parameters will be set and tested by your vet, so be sure to get your aging dog checked every six months.

5. Prevent Them from Escaping

Dogs love exploring their surroundings, even if the experience is not very beneficial for them. Because you are a concerned owner, you want your dog to remain safe even without physical confinement. The fact is that roaming dogs not only challenge objects kept inside your home, but have strong temptations to jump over the physical barriers you have in your backyard.

You may feel that restricting your dog's freedom is not the right thing to do, but remember your pet can get injured or harm others if let free. One of the best features that make an in-ground containment system so popular is the fact that your dog can still roam about freely – but only within the allowable boundaries. This without doubt is a much better solution than building tortuous physical barriers to confine your pet.

While dogs can be kept confined in one place, they are healthier if you give them a chance to run and exercise outdoors. Chaining your pet to one spot is only a short-term solution. You cannot expect your pet to sit in one place while you can move around anywhere you like. Long-term leash or chain confinement is not only cruel, but also puts your pet under a great deal of stress.

The only thing you need to keep in mind is that stressed animals can get extremely aggressive. And if your pet gets a chance to escape, it can harm you or other people around. If you have decided to keep a dog, remember that this newcomer needs a little bit of training to become a good and obedient pet.

Before you leave the young pup outside your home, you must make sure that your pet's imagination is not running wild. Forget the scratches that are prominent on your couches and carpets, you have to prevent your curious companion from jumping over the tall fence and landing in front of a speedy car.

Dogs can get bored very easily and therefore they may escape to find some adventure or job to do. This is also the case with Caucasian Shepherds. Other reasons why dogs may escape is loneliness, if they are left alone for too long; separation anxiety; territory protection – Caucasians may lose track of the way while chasing intruders away; and then there's prey intrusion in which dogs may veer away further than is good for them while hunting and chasing after their prey.

Dog escapes can be prevented by the following ways:

1- Training your dog not to bolt out from doors and exits
2- Making sure your property is fenced and secure
3- Provide daily activities to redirect and drain the dog's energy
4- Reward the dog for staying in the house or the property
5- Teaching the dog proper guarding behavior – that is, not going further than a certain limit away from home boundary.

6. What to do when the dog attacks someone?

Territorial Aggression:

For a dog like the Caucasian Shepherd that is territorially aggressive, guarding their home is a common characteristic and almost an instinct. As these puppies grow into adult dogs, they guard the yard and the home as well as the car they are used to travelling in. It is this territorial aggression that gets the mailman and any other service providers or guests bitten.

This territorial aggression is a prized instinct in guard dogs like the Caucasian Shepherd as well as Rottweilers and Akitas. Hence, if you do not want such an aggression in your pet, do not get this breed. But if you do happen to have it, then you must dominate the dog and make you are the leader of the pack. The 'alpha' role must be assumed by the owner, and not the dog. Becoming the leader of the pack is the first step in making the dog obeys you. You set the rules and decide who is a friend and who is an enemy. You should train it in a way that it looks to you for advice when a stranger approaches it. If you have cooperating friends, ask them to help you train the dog by approaching the house and then letting you socialize the dog with them. They can also feed the dog with treats cautiously and may be even taking the dog for a walk on a leash. You must fence your yard so that the limits of the territory are clear to the dog.

Predatory Aggression:
Dogs like the Caucasian Shepherd, Australian Shepherd, healers and border colliers have an instinctive drive to worry, chase and even nip. It will take a lot of effort on their own part not to herd the children of the family also. The solution to containing this instinct of the dog is to ensure that every member of the family has done obedience training of the dog, especially the children. These dogs are very loving but they just have this natural urge to herd and boss around. You can overcome this problem if you make the dog understand that this behavior is a problem and hence, unacceptable. A strong reprimand and a stern 'NO!' should usually suffice. You may have to keep reminding them of the rules. Your dog will probably not display this behavior when it is on a short leash.

What to do when your dog does bite?
If your dog bites someone, the first thing to do is to not be shocked or panicked. But, it is essential that you take swift action if a dog does bite you or someone else. Follow the following steps:

1- Remain calm and do not panic
2- Restrict your dog to one room or to his crate
3- Make the bite victim wash the wound properly with soap and warm water
4- Treat the victim with courtesy and sympathy. Do not get defensive or lay blame. Anything you say can be used against you later in civil or legal action.

115

5- A medical expert should be contacted for the victim. If the bite is too severe, an ambulance may be needed.

6- Get the victim's contact information and give him yours. You might need to give him your insurance information in case it is needed.

7- Obtain the contact information of any witnesses.

8- Get in touch with your veterinarian and take your dog's medical records from him.

9- Inform any local authority on the incident and comply with their orders.

You might need to show your dog's rabies vaccination history and accordingly a quarantine period may be required. Depending on the history of your dog and the bite intensity, your dog may be designated a 'dangerous dog' label. Following this, you will have to follow any and all orders regarding the handling of your dog. Your dog may even be euthanized if it is too dangerous, i.e. the bite was too dangerous or if a fatality had occurred. You might even be held legally responsible and may even face criminal charges.

After the victim has been bitten, offer to pay medical expenses even though it is not legally ordered. To prevent such incidences in the future, contact a professional trainer and maybe even a veterinary behaviorist.

Some Useful Websites

Below are a few websites that you can visit and find them useful while caring for your Caucasian Shepherd. They have a wealth of knowledge pertaining to grooming and obedience training of your Caucasian Shepherd.

1- http://www.vetstreet.com
2- http://www.dogbreedinfo.com
3- http://www.dog-breeds-expert.com

With respect to feeding your dog, the following website is especially helpful:

http://vbocaucasian.com/feeding-a-puppy.html

If you wish to buy a Caucasian Shepherd puppy in the UK, then visit the link below:

http://www.europuppy.com

If you are looking for a dog in the US, then visit:

http://www.petfinder.com

For dog clubs that may provide a wealth of knowledge about petting your dog, the following websites will come in handy:

For USA:

American Kennel Clubs: http://www.akc.org/

Kennel Club USA: http://www.kennelclubusa.com/

For UK:

Dog Club UK: http://www.dogclub.co.uk

The Kennel Club UK: www.thekennelclub.org.uk

In case of emergencies, or abuse reporting, you call contact the below:

For US:

ASPCA: http://www.aspca.org/

The Humane Society: http://www.humanesociety.org/

For UK:

Rspca: http://www.rspca.org.uk/home

Humane Society International International: http://www.hsi.org

For breeding:

In USA:

American Dog Breeders Association: http://www.adba.cc/

Pure Bred Breeders: http://purebredbreeders.com/

In UK:

Breeders Online: http://www.breedersonline.co.uk/

Eurobreeder: http://www.eurobreeder.com

Useful Checklists

Check the appropriate checklist below after you have achieved a certain goal in the grooming, training and feeding of your Caucasian Shepherd Dog:

Diet	
Providing high quality food – avoiding chocolate, corn, wheat, by products, artificial preservatives, boiled bones and those with artificial colors	
Adding fresh and healthy supplements to food like fresh vegetables and meat; yoghurt	
Avoid giving it junk food	

Handling and Grooming	
Dog is comfortable with being touched on ears, tail, feet and you ensure this on a daily basis	
It is comfortable with combing or brushing	
It is frequently brushed and that prevents matting of the coat and keeps skin healthy	
It is comfortable with ear cleaning	
Ears are cleaned weekly	
Dog is comfortable with brushing its teeth	
Its teeth are brushed weekly	
Dog is comfortable with being bathed	
It is bathed once a month	

Exercise and Play	
Your dog has many toys	
It is addicted to at least one of them	
It gets 30 minutes of exercise every day with a person	
It gets 10 minutes of training a day	

For proper socialization, make note of following:	
Your dog is comfortable with male and female adults	
It is comfortable with male and female children	
It is comfortable with people that have special needs (wheelchairs, crutches, etc)	

To prevent possessiveness, make note of following:	
It is comfortable with others touching its bed, food bowl or toys	
It is comfortable with sharing its best friend with other people	

For comfortable car rides	
It is comfortable riding in a car	
It is restrained amply in the car	

Miscellaneous requirements	
It gets at least 10 hours of sleep every day	
It visits the vet regularly and gets distemper and rabies vaccination	
It is spayed or neutered	
It has proper weight – the ribs can be felt are not distended	
It is not left outside for long hours	
It seldom has any housetraining accidents – maybe just 1 a week	
Any excess vaccinations or parasite treatments are avoided	

Conclusion

The Caucasian Shepherd dog breed is a majestic one. It is big, it is stubborn but it makes a very loyal companion. Surely such a dog cannot be reared without a little pain. As the Book showed you, you have to be very particular about most aspects of its rearing – be it feeding, training, socialization, vet care, etc. If you follow all the rules outlined to the letter, you are all set to be training a companion for life. They will guard you, your property and your family with the best of its abilities and ensure that no one hurts them. But slack off a little in keeping an eye on it, and socializing it, and you will find mauled friends and neighbors who made a grave mistake of stepping on your property without your supervision.

There are a lot of controversies surrounding this breed, and most of them are baseless and wrong. The Caucasian Shepherds are great dogs and will prove to be a great investment of your time and money if you follow all the guidelines provided in this Book.

We hope you enjoyed reading this book and found everything you needed to find with respective to keeping a Caucasian Shepherd as a pet.

Published by IMB Publishing 2014